Moondyne Joe

THE MAN AND THE MYTH

Moondyne Joe

THE MAN AND THE MYTH

Ian Elliot

UNIVERSITY OF WESTERN AUSTRALIA PRESS

1978

First published in 1978 by
University of Western Australia Press
Nedlands, Western Australia

Eastern states of Australia, New Zealand, Papua and New Guinea:
Melbourne University Press, PO Box 278, Carlton South, Vict. 3053

UK, Europe, Middle East, Africa, the Caribbean:
International Scholarly Book Services (Europe),
8 Willian Way, Letchworth, Hartfordshire SG6 2HG, England

USA, its territories and possessions, Canada:
International Scholarly Book Services, Inc.
Box 555, Forest Grove, Oregon 97116, USA

Elliot, Ian Andrew, 1943-
Moondyne Joe.

Index.
Bibliography.
ISBN 0 85564 130 4.

1. Johns, Joseph Bolitho. 2. Bush-rangers —
Biography. I. Title.

364.155'0994[1]

Set in Baskerville 10/12 by University of Western Australia Press
Printed and bound by Silex Enterprise & Printing Co., Hong Kong

Acknowledgements

My thanks are due to the following people.

The staff of the Battye Library for their unfailing interest and assistance which makes research into any facet of Western Australian history a pleasant and rewarding experience.

The Commissioner of Police for permission to make use of police records held by the Battye Library.

The Director of the Department of Corrections for permission to examine convict records held by the Battye Library, also for permission to inspect and photograph Moondyne Joe's cell in Fremantle Prison.

Warder A. Stewart who conducted me on my first guided tour of Fremantle Prison.

Mr J. R. Driscoll, Assistant Director (Institutions) and Mr J. L. Bunn, Superintendent of Fremantle Prison, who made possible a hurried return visit to the prison for additional material prior to publication.

Mr and Mrs W. E. Taylor of 'Lady Spring', South Chittering, for permission to visit the site of Bassett's capture on their property.

Mr K. Edwards of 'Moondyne' for permission to visit Moondyne Spring and the surrounding area on several occasions.

My father, Mr A. W. Elliot, for his company and photography on several field trips.

Miss Pippa Spatcher who assisted with research and braved bush tracks, thorn bushes and kangaroo tick to accompany me on the first unsuccessful attempt to locate Joe's Cage in the 'Moondyne Hills'.

Mr Campbell Cornish for his photography and for preparing a map to accompany the manuscript and linocuts for chapter headings.

My wife, Susan, and Mrs Rhelma Symonds for their assistance in typing the manuscript.

Mrs Connie Miller and Mr John Keating for their advice and all others who assisted in any way, especially those friends whose constant interest and encouragement meant so much.

Ian Elliot
Glen Forrest 1977

Contents

Illustrations

Introduction

Bushrangers are the Australian equivalent of English highwaymen and American outlaws. All of these considered that the world owed them a living. Most early bushrangers were transported convicts who escaped and 'ranged the bush' taking whatever came their way. Later the gold-rush days of Victoria and New South Wales saw a new breed of bushranger. Men born and bred in the colonies took advantage of the lucrative roadside pickings.

The first bushranger of note was 'Black' Caesar, an escaped convict who was robbing settlers on the outskirts of Sydney before that settlement was two years old. In later years 'Bold' Jack Donahoe (the original Wild Colonial Boy), 'Darkey' Underwood, William Westwood or 'Jackey Jackey' (the Dick Turpin of bushranging), and others, became part of Australia's folklore by their bushranging exploits. But the decade from 1860 to 1870 became the classic period of bushranging. Throughout those years the romantic figures of Frank Gardiner (King of the Road), Ben Hall and his gang, Fred Ward (Thunderbolt) and the notorious Clarke brothers became legendary. These men made large hauls from gold-laden coaches and made a laughing stock of the police and governments of their time. Thieves and murderers they may have been, but their daring exploits made them heroes amongst the impoverished, outlying free-selectors or 'cockies'. A colonial observer of the period noted the reluctance of schoolboys to take the part of a policeman when the game of bushrangers was to be played, and it is the bushrangers, not the police who hunted them, who have become our folk heroes.

Goldfields were not discovered in Western Australia until after
the advent of railways and telegraphic communications, and as a
result our goldrushes did not have the problems with marauding
bushrangers that plagued other states. In spite of this the state has a
rich heritage of bushranging tales from the convict era, about which
very little has been written. Western Australia's best known bushranger, Moondyne Joe, became prominent during Governor Hampton's unpopular rule in the 1860s, and this book is an attempt to
portray his career accurately and correct some of the misconceptions
which have arisen in later years. Some writers have given the impression that Joe was Western Australia's 'only' bushranger and this idea
is now widespread. To show the absurdity of such a notion, the
exploits of a good many of Western Australia's bushrangers were
deliberately included in this work. There can be little doubt that
Joe was influenced by the exploits of some and no doubt that his
actions influenced many.

Joe's career is not as spectacular as those of his eastern contemporaries. His robberies were mostly trifling and he rarely resorted to
violence. This seems to have endeared him to the settlers, few of
whom appear to have feared him. His prison sentences were frequently punctuated by escapes, to the discomfiture of the governor
and his son, the acting comptroller-general, and the corresponding
delight of the press. The Western Australian police spared no effort
to recapture Joe after his escapes. The daily journals of officers
engaged in his pursuit were preserved in the state archives in the
State Reference Library by the forethought of Mr Cecil Treadgold,
secretary of the Police Department from 1919 to 1945. They make
fascinating reading and have contributed a great deal to the compiling of this book. All extracts quoted from such journals retain
the original spelling and punctuation, i.e. are reproduced *verbatim
et litteratim.*

During his sojourns in prison Joe himself was a prolific letter
writer. He wrote frequently to the authorities protesting his innocence and requesting remissions, but none of this correspondence
appears to have survived. All that remains in the Convict Establishment Letterbooks are brief notes on the contents of letters sent and
the answers given. These rarely exceed one line and give no clue to
the arguments put forward or the reasoning behind them. Denied

this avenue of insight into the man's personality, I have found it difficult to portray adequately the real Joe whose character can only be guessed at from his actions.

Bushranging in Western Australia took place in the days when Aboriginal trackers were an integral part of the police force, when a horse was a man's best friend and bushmanship was the measure of a man. Joe became a legend in his own time because of his ingenious escapes and his outstanding bushmanship. He deserves his place in Australian folklore, but those who speak of him should have access to the true story and that is the purpose of this book.

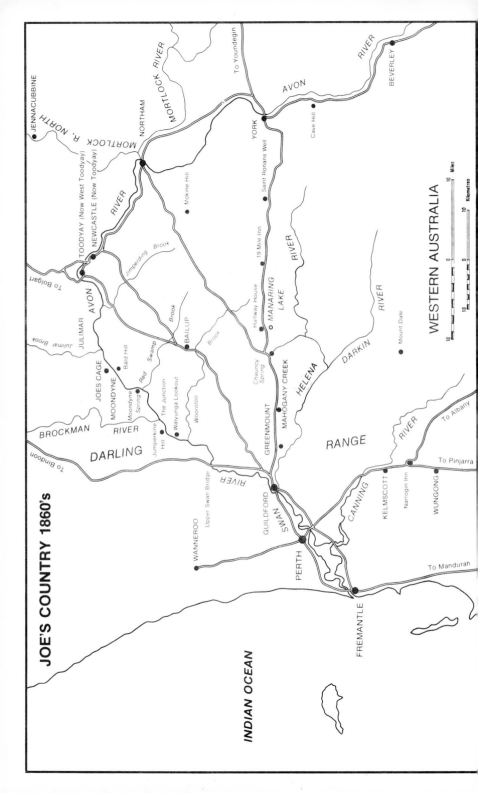

JOE'S COUNTRY 1860's

WESTERN AUSTRALIA

INDIAN OCEAN

JENNACUBBINE

MORTLOCK R. NORTH

MORTLOCK RIVER

To Youndegin

AVON RIVER

BEVERLEY

NORTHAM

York

Cave Hill

Mokine Hill

Saint Ronans Well

TOODYAY (Now West Toodyay)

NEWCASTLE (Now Toodyay)

RIVER

To Bolgart

Jimperding Brook

19 Mile Inn

AVON

JULIMAR

Julimar Brook

Brook

BAILUP

Brook

Halfway House

MANARING

LAKE

RIVER

JOES CAGE

MOONDYNE

Bald Hill

Red Swamp

The Junction

Chauncy Spring

MAHOGANY CREEK

HELENA

DARKIN RIVER

Mount Dale

Moondyne Spring

Waiyunga Lookout

Wooroloo

GREENMOUNT

BROCKMAN RIVER

Jumperkine Hill

To Bindoon

DARLING RANGE

Upper Swan Bridge

RIVER

GUILDFORD

SWAN

CANNING RIVER

To Albany

KELMSCOTT

Narrogin Inn

To Pinjarra

WUNGONG

WANNEROO

PERTH

To Mandurah

FREMANTLE

Miles

Kilometres

Chapter
one

1848-1853

At about 2.30 am on a cold November night in 1848 two young men, each with a bag over his shoulder, trudged towards the village of Monmouth in Wales. Their stride checked momentarily as they became aware of the shadowy figure of a policeman standing in the roadway ahead, but, with possibly a nudge and a low-muttered word, they continued towards him. Not entirely unexpectedly, his challenge rang out as they came up to him. In reply to his questioning they stated that they came from Ross and were on their way to Chepstow. As luck would have it, the road they were on came from the direction of Llanelly, not Ross, and this slip led Sergeant William Fuller to question them further. He found their answers as to the contents of the bags 'unsatisfactory' and marched them to a nearby house where the bags were taken from them and opened. Out rolled several cheeses, three loaves of bread (one partly eaten), two pieces of bacon, part of a shoulder of mutton and piece of suet. The sergeant immediately took the pair into custody on suspicion of theft.[1]

The prisoners proved to be William Cross, a labourer with one previous conviction, and a young man named Joseph Bolitho Johns. For the latter this first brush with the law was to be the beginning of a long and eventful association. Later he would become known as 'Moondyne Joe', a 'good' badman who gallops across the pages of Western Australian history with all the wild free spirit of a wiry bush brumby. Around his name have been woven so many tall tales and campfire yarns that the real story is difficult to unravel. His early days remain almost a complete mystery. His father, Thomas Johns, was a blacksmith, but the exact year of Joe's birth has yet to be established, one source suggesting 1826 and another 1828.[2] Also unknown is his nationality. Although he is usually assumed to be Welsh, probably because of his arrest at Monmouth in his early twenties, surely only strangers would have made the slip on road directions mentioned above. A later description tells us that he was 1.80 metre (5 feet 10¾ inches) in height, had black hair, hazel eyes, a long visage, sallow complexion and a pock-pitted appearance, the latter no doubt the result of contracting smallpox in his youth. He was of the Roman Catholic faith and a miner by trade.[3]

Within a day or two of their arrest, the news arrived that goods answering the description of those found in the prisoners' possession had been reported stolen from the house of Richard Price of Llanelly, Breconshire, the day previous to their being apprehended. They were promptly charged with the theft. They attended a preliminary hearing at Crickhowell and finally went on trial at Llanelly in March 1849. They conducted their own defence with a considerable amount of cheek, Joe showing himself to be articulate and quick-witted in questioning the prosecution witnesses.[4]

Elizabeth Phillips, Price's housekeeper, was the first witness to be called. She recollected going to bed on Monday 13 November soon after 10.00 pm. The doors were all fastened then, but when she came downstairs the following morning about 7.00 am, the dairy and back door were both open and she missed some bread, several cheeses, part of a shoulder of mutton and a piece of bacon. There was a hole in the window large enough, in her opinion, for a person to get through. After Mr T. Allen, who held the brief for the prosecution, had completed his questioning of the witness, several rather meaningless questions were put by Cross. Joe asked only two questions.

'Were you the first to go downstairs that morning?'

'Yes.'

'What time was that?'

'About seven o-clock.'

The next witness was Price himself who recalled getting home about 10.00 pm on that night. His housekeeper had locked the front door behind him, and he had retired upstairs to bed shortly afterwards. During the night he had heard something like a jug fall on the floor, and when he came down in the morning, his house-keeper, who was down first, had directed his attention to the broken window near which he saw a broken blacking jar which might have caused the noise. He noticed missing a quantity of bread, cheese and bacon and part of a shoulder of mutton.

As soon as Mr Allen had regained his seat Joe was speaking: 'Did you not say at Crickhowell that, in consequence of the noise you heard in the morning, you called your man-servant to see what was the matter?'

Price replied that he called his servant to go and see after the cows, which he did, but the man went out at the front door and could not see anything that might have occurred at the back of the house.

'The previous witness swore just now that she was down first', Joe remarked acidly. 'Now it appears that your servant was the first person down.'

Flustered, Price replied that the servant had only been down for about half an hour and had returned to bed as soon as he had seen after the cows.

Noticing frowns on the faces of several of the jury, a momentarily worried Mr Allen immediately re-examined, eliciting the information that Price considered the hole in the window large enough to admit a boy, having himself put a boy through in order to ascertain the fact. Price was then allowed to step down.

His place was taken by Sergeant Fuller who related his story. Both prisoners did their best to discredit Fuller, suggesting that he did not hear their replies correctly on the night of their arrest and that he was drunk at the time. They made very little headway. The experienced police officer parried their insinuations calmly and obviously made a good impression on the jury.

The prisoner's fate was sealed when the goods found on them were produced in court and identified by both Elizabeth Phillips and her employer. The judge summed up the case and the jury returned a verdict of guilty almost immediately. Both prisoners were sentenced to ten years' transportation and returned to their cells. The fate of Cross is unknown; Joe was to wait four long years before orders for his removal to a convict colony finally came through.

In the meantime, by an order of Her Majesty Queen Victoria, acting on the advice of her Privy Council at Buckingham Palace on 1 May 1849, Western Australia was nominated as one of those colonies to which felons and other offenders under sentence or order of transportation or banishment could be conveyed.[5] Strangely, at a time when all other colonies were strenuously objecting to convicts, this order was the result of a request from the Western Australian colonists who had been strongly advocating transportation for some years past. Twenty years earlier, when the colony was founded, a pledge had been given by the British Government that convicts would not be sent to the new settlement.[6] Now however, a shortage of labour was crippling the economy, and it was considered by many that the introduction of convicts on a large scale, with imperial funds to match, was the only means left of placing the colony in a prosperous condition.[7]

The first convict ship, the barque *Scindian*, arrived at Fremantle on 1 June 1850, bearing seventy-five convicts and fifty pensioner guards as well as other passengers, mostly the wives and children of the guards. They found the colony totally unprepared for them and were temporarily lodged in rented premises while they began the work of building the Fremantle Prison, originally called the Convict Establishment, in which later arrivals were confined.[8] Other convict ships arrived at intervals, and by the end of the year various other public works were under construction, and depots for ticket-of-leave men were being established in several country centres.[9]

A ticket of leave was granted to convicts who had served a period of probation and had proved by their good behaviour that they could be allowed a certain amount of liberty. A ticket-of-leave man was free to seek employment in an assigned district, but was not permitted to leave it without the consent of the comptroller-general of convicts or the resident magistrate of the district assigned. From the depot the convicts were hired by settlers or employed on public works such as the construction of roads or bridges. From his wages the ticket-of-leave man was compelled to repay the comptroller-general the sum of £15, this being the cost of his passage to the colony. Every change of master or residence was endorsed on his ticket — unfortunately very few of these documents have survived the years and this means of tracing movements of ticket-of-leave men is denied to the historian. Well-conducted ticket-of-leave men were permitted to marry or to bring their wives and families from England at half cost. They could also acquire property, but if guilty of any misconduct, could be arrested without warrant and would forfeit such property to the Crown. They could be summarily tried without recourse to the Supreme Court and were not allowed to carry fire-arms or board a ship without special permission.

A convict who observed the conditions of his ticket of leave until the completion of one half of his original sentence became entitled to a conditional pardon which removed all restrictions except the right to leave the state until the whole term of his sentence had expired.[10]

During ensuing years a steady stream of convicts entered the colony, and eventually Joe, as convict number 1790, was marched aboard the 832-ton *Pyrenees* commanded by Captain Freeman.[11] As had been the case with the other 295 convicts crammed on board, Joe's good behaviour had earned him an immediate ticket of leave upon arrival in the Colony of Western Australia, for which the ship was bound. In addition to the convicts, who were under the care of Surgeon Superintendent Bowers, the ship carried 2 religious instructors, 29 pensioner guards, 24 women and 40 children, as well as her officers and crew. She sailed from Portsmouth on 2 February 1853.[12] The voyage was probably not as arduous for the convicts as might be imagined. Many reforms had been made since the bad old days of New South Wales and Van Diemen's Land, when convicts were chained below the decks of ex-slavers for the entire voyage, lolling in their own filth, with death by any number of diseases a constant companion. The ship that carried Joe was large, clean and a fast sailer. The prisoners were allowed on deck, and, with the prospect of comparative freedom at their eventual destinations, most would have been relatively happy and well-behaved. New friend-

1 The gates of Fremantle Prison

ships would have been formed and perhaps old acquaintances re-
newed. On a previous voyage of the *Pyrenees*, carrying convicts
between England and Western Australia, it was recorded that the
convicts 'were an orderly, well behaved body of men and during
fine weather made the evenings pleasant by their songs and good
humoured revelry'.[13] No doubt things were much the same during
Joe's voyage. In fact, as later events proved, the prisoners' lot was
envied by many of the crew, amongst whom the rumour had cir-
culated that gold had been discovered in the colony. Eighteen crew
members went on strike shortly after the vessel had arrived and
were conveyed to gaol.[14] They must have been annoyed to find the
rumour false.

   The *Pyrenees* anchored in Cockburn Sound on Saturday 30 April
1853 and on the following day the prisoners were brought on deck
in batches to be issued with their tickets of leave.[15] Whilst on deck
Joe would have gazed curiously towards the shores of his new home-
land. The low and uninviting coastline was topped by the distant
blue of the hills he would come to love. In the foreground, Fremantle, the colony's port, was a huddle of limestone houses glaring
white in the sun. It was not a large settlement. Years earlier a

quartermaster of one of His Majesty's ships had disparagingly suggested that the whole town could be run through an hour-glass in a day. The unpaved street, of sand had been edged with clay footpaths since then, but still the drifting sand dismayed newcomers. Although the port was situated at the mouth of the Swan River, a rock bar closed the entrance. Cargoes had to be landed by lighter at South Beach and transported by road to a wharf on the river before going on to Perth. On a rise behind Fremantle spread the partly-completed Convict Establishment, dominating the entire scene. Joe could have had no inkling that his use of those grim prison gates more often as an entrance than an exit would eventually thrust him into the folklore of this young colony.

REFERENCES

1. *Hereford Times* 31 March 1849.
2. Mary Tamblyn, Research in 1968, WAA 2086A.
3. Convict Records, WAA Acc No. 1156 R4.
4. *Hereford Times* 31 March 1849.
5. *Government Gazette* 6 November 1849, p. 2.
6. J. S. Battye, *Western Australia: A History from its Discovery to the Inauguration of the Commonwealth* (Oxford: Oxford University Press 1924), p. 76.
7. Ibid p. 201.
8. Ibid p. 207.
9. Ibid p. 209.
10. *Government Gazette* 8 April 1851, p. 3.
11. Convict Records, WAA Acc. No. 1156 R20.
12. *Inquirer* 4 May 1853; *Perth Gazette* 6 May 1853.
13. J. T. Reilly, *Reminiscences of Fifty Years Residence in Western Australia* (Perth: Sands & McDougall 1901), p. 4.
14. *Inquirer* 11 May 1853.
15. Convict Records, WAA Acc. No. 1156 R21B.

Chapter two

1853-1861

It has proved impossible to trace Joe's life during his first years in the colony. Groups of ticket-of-leave men from the *Pyrenees* were despatched to various centres, the first party leaving for York only five days after the arrival of the ship.[1] Others were included in a draft of men proceeding to Port Gregory,[2] a small reef-sheltered harbour about 630 kilometres to the north of Fremantle, which had recently achieved prominence because of its proximity to the newly-established Geraldine Lead Mine. Plans were afoot at that time to repair the old colonial schooner *Champion* to be used as a floating convict depot at Port Gregory, but eventually a board of survey recommended that she be broken up and sold.[3]

The Port Gregory party embarked on the brigantine *Leander* which after many delays sailed on Saturday 14 May 1853.[4] Much concern was expressed for the welfare of those aboard who were to remain in the new settlement without the benefit of a medical officer.[5] On arrival at the port Captain Johnston sailed his ship safely through the passage now bearing her name and anchored her close to the beach for unloading. During the *Leander*'s stay the cutter *Gold Digger* entered the port by another passage, now known as Gold Digger Passage, and 'the circumstances of there being two vessels in the harbour for the first time was celebrated by the *Leander* being dressed in flags and some little jollity taking place.'[6] Knowing Joe to have had mining experience, it is tempting to assume that he was a part of the pioneer group at Port Gregory that day but no proof exists.

Forty *Pyrenees* convicts were stationed at the foot of Mount Eliza and work recommenced on the construction of what is now Mounts Bay Road. Others were sent to the Toodyay depot,[7] and in view of Joe's settling near there later, it is possible that he was amongst this batch. The remainder sailed for Bunbury and King George Sound aboard the *William Pope*, or were put to work clearing the road to Albany.[8] Those at the depots were employed on road clearing or other public works until engaged by private masters, usually farmers.

Not long after Joe's arrival great consternation was caused in the colony by a speech of Lord John Russell delivered in the House of

2 'The Junction' from Walyunga Lookout

Commons, which gave the impression that no further convicts were
to be sent to Western Australia. Having grown accustomed to this
ready source of cheap labour, the settlers were horrified at the
thought of doing without it, and much discussion and many meetings
took place before it was discovered that Lord Russell had meant no
such thing.[9]

Wherever Joe worked and whoever he worked for, he appears to
have stayed out of trouble. A conditional pardon was granted to
him on 10 March 1855.[10] During his next six years of freedom Joe
became an expert bushman. He settled in one of the wildest and
most inaccessible places in the Darling Range, the steep, rugged
valley through which the Avon River winds to meet Wooroloo Brook
and become the Swan. The country on the north side of this valley
was known to the Aborigines as 'Moondyne', the Brockman River in
those days was usually called 'Chittering Brook', and the spot where
it merges with the Avon River, near Jumperkine Hill, was known as
'The Junction'.

Joe made his living by partly fencing the numerous springs in the
area and trapping stray cattle and horses that came to drink. These
horse traps were strongly and skilfully constructed. One of the them,
situated at a spring near the head of Joes Brook, was considered a
significant landmark by surveyor G. H. Roe in 1867 and was shown
on maps as Joes Cage. The author visited this wild and lonely spot
several times in 1975-76 and finally located the remains of the trap.
After nearly 120 years and despite the ravages of fire and termites,
three posts were still standing, bearing mute testimony to Joe's work-
manship. There was no evidence of wire or nails having been used.
The 30-centimetre diameter posts stood about 2.44 metres high and
the same distance apart and were notched to support five horizontal
rails. The whole structure originally measured 20 metres long by 10
metres wide. Unfortunately, although the surviving posts are within
the Avon Valley National Park, there is little chance of protection
from the bushfires that periodically sweep these hills, and no doubt
these last remaining traces of Joe's presence will eventually disappear.

Joe's life in this wild and remote region was rough but at least a
man was his own boss, a circumstance of no small value to an
ex-convict. The life was not as lonely as one might imagine. Although no settlers had taken up land in the more rugged areas

3 Joes Cage: two of the posts still standing

4 Joes Cage: a corner post of the stockyard

5 The spring near Joes Cage

frequented by Joe, they often visited the place in search of lost stock. It would have been natural for them to enquire whether Joe had sighted the objects of their search and perhaps to offer him a reward for their recapture.

Joe was not the only man engaged in trapping stock in the area. Another was James Everett who ran the Queen's Head Hotel in Toodyay. Everett was not well liked and the police were continually suspicious of him, keeping a close watch on his trapping activities.[11] He and Joe were enemies, but as there were others besides Joe and Everett who trapped along the river, it is doubtful that Joe had any real lack of companionship in spite of the comparative isolation of his home. Indeed, if he ever became really lonely, it was only a 19-kilometre ride from Moondyne Spring, up Red Swamp Brook, to the wayside inn at Bailup, where he could drink and yarn with the teamsters and sawyers who frequented the place—men of his own class who would have respected him for his independent spirit and knowledge of bushcraft. From about the time of Joe's conditional pardon in 1855 this inn was run for some years by William McKnoe, but in early 1860 the license was taken over by Robert Wheeler,[12] who put a man named Fitzgerald in charge of the place.[13] As becomes obvious later, Joe was also a frequent visitor to a sawyer's camp situated about 3 kilometres north-east of Bailup, and no doubt he also often visited Toodyay itself, which, during this period, boasted three hotels, Everett's Queen's Head, John Herbert's Royal Oak and another run by Alexander Warren. The town of Toodyay was then situated at what is now known as West Toodyay. As the place was subject to flooding, in the early 1860s a new town was surveyed about 3 kilometres south-east. This was named Newcastle, and it is referred to as such throughout this book although the name was changed to Toodyay in 1911.

In 1858 Warren sold his hotel to Isaac Doust and moved to a property on the road between Guildford and Bindoon, where he established a small wayside tavern called the 'Bush Inn'.[14] This was about 19 kilometres west of Moondyne Spring and was well known to Joe.

Joe gave a sense of permanency to his camp at Moondyne by building some rough bush huts there, which afforded him shelter and gave him a place to store his few belongings.[15] The precise location of these huts is difficult to establish. A search around Moondyne Spring itself in 1976 failed to reveal traces of buildings, although a piece of old timber found lying in the bracken by the owner of the property, Mr Ken Edwards, was clearly notched to take a stockyard rail. This is probably all that remains of the large horse trap built by Joe at the spring. Old timers of the district talk of a ruined hut near the junction of Moondyne Brook and the Avon River and another on the south side of the river. While it is possible that either of these could be the remains of Joe's camp, it seems more logical to assume that the camp was not far from Moondyne Spring. On the main branch of Moondyne Brook, only a few hundred metres from the spring, is an unusual rock formation over which the stream flows, falling vertically some 3 metres before splashing onto a flat rock below. In the 1960s this was used as a shower by the Edwards family, and it is not hard to imagine Joe using it for the same purpose one hundred years earlier.

In November 1860 a man whose career may have had some influence on Joe's subsequent actions passed through the Moondyne country. This was James Lilly who, like Joe, had been transported to Western Australia as a convict. Later he had been reconvicted in the colony for horse stealing,[16] and, while serving his sentence, had escaped from Fremantle and committed several holdups and thefts around Toodyay before being recaptured.[17] Released on a ticket of leave in 1860, he found work on the Canning, but was again accused of horse stealing and promptly took to the bush.[18] At about the same time a man named Frank Hall, charged with cattle stealing at the Vasse, also absconded. The hue and cry after Hall was great. Sir Alexander Campbell, the superintendent of police, visiting a friend at Capel, mistook a respectable settler for Hall and had him chained up, an embarrassing affair, and one that could have influenced Campbell's resignation soon afterward.[19]

Unlike Hall, who was never sighted after his escape, Lilly was seen frequently near York. One of his better known exploits was selling a stolen horse to a shepherd, using the money to buy a pair of revolvers, with which he then held up the shepherd and demanded the horse back.[20] On the morning of Saturday 13 October 1860 Lilly approached the house of J. Whitnell and John Woods armed with one of his six-barrelled revolvers, a common weapon of the period. He told them that Frank Hall had died in his arms the previous evening and offered to take them to the body. They agreed to accompany him the following day and, in the meantime, sent in a report to the government resident at York, Mr L. Bayley, who immediately notified Sergeant Thomas Bailey in charge of the York police station.

Mounted Constables Regan and Edwards were sent out to ascertain whether any truth was attached to the story, and to apprehend Lilly. The 55-kilometre journey took them until 1.00 pm on the Sunday, by which time Lilly's story had been found to be a hoax and the runaway had disappeared.[21] Lilly's motives are obscure although one report in a contemporary newspaper stated that after luring Whitnell and Woods into the bush to see the supposed body he gave them the slip, doubled back and stole one of their horses.[22] At all events he led Police Constable William Regan a merry dance from this time on. On the 20th he became news again when he demanded two days' provisions from Mr S. S. Parker's shepherd, but because a fair was in progress at York, no more police could be spared to join the search.[23] Reinforcements were sent two days later when it was heard that Mr Quartermaine had been forced at gunpoint to hand over his horse to Lilly.[24] The excellent job being done by Regan and his tracker can be judged by the fact that they arrived at Quartermaine's homestead only two hours behind Lilly, but again the bushranger escaped.[25] Continually stealing fresh horses, Lilly could move much faster than the police, who were besieged by reports coming in from all directions from settlers claiming to have sighted the fugitive.

On 25 October a report was sent to the superintendent of police from Guildford, stating that it had been heard that Lilly had taken from the constables who were on his tracks their two horses, their arms and handcuffed them. This was supposed to have taken place near Mr John Spice's place on the 'Chittering Brook', not far from Moondyne. Whether this report was true or not it resulted in the Guildford police joining in the now intensive manhunt for five days, but they too searched without success.[26]

Police Constable Regan stayed on the trail for two and a half weeks until the 30th, when the tracks were lost at Moondyne. Could this be more than just a coincidence? The thing that makes one

wonder is that, although Regan and his tracker, an excellent team
as we have seen, searched the locality diligently for tracks before
they gave up and returned to York, Lilly apparently stayed at or
near Moondyne for almost a week at this time. On the afternoon of
Sunday 4 November Lilly walked boldly into the Bailup Inn tap
room, placed a revolver at Fitzgerald's heart and asked if any police
were about. Fitzgerald replied in the negative and Lilly demanded
a glass of grog with which he was supplied. He remarked that there
did not seem to be many travellers about that afternoon and told
the hostler to take care of a kangaroo dog bitch for him, as she was
knocked up and hindering his progress. He then strode out, but
returned five minutes later on a grey horse upon which he sat
outside for about ten minutes before galloping off in the direction
of Moondyne. It is obvious that this appearance was meant to bring
the police racing back to Moondyne, whilst Lilly headed for other
parts, but in this he was unsuccessful. The news took four days to
reach Guildford, and the result was the suggestion of a ruse which
would later be tried on Joe. It was decided to disguise a police
officer and get him a job at Bailup to await a return visit of Lilly.
Police Constable McAlinden of Fremantle was selected for the
scheme, but by the time he reached Bailup, Lilly was already in
custody.[27]

About this time, just before his capture, Lilly wrote to the *Inquirer*. His letter was published on 7 November and read [*verbatim*]:

> I, James Lilly, wish to inform the settlers of my going into the bush,
> through Henry Mead asserting at the Police Station, on the Canning,
> and brought accusations against me for stealing his horse and calling
> me a — — convict in the presence of the policemans wife and family
> and several more besides in the district which I could not bear, and
> forced me to the bush and take up arms, and I do not intend doing
> any harm at present, if His Excellency be pleased to allow me to go
> to my friends in another colony, and what I have done I will restore
> to everyone uninjured, and, if not, would sooner die than come in
> out of the bush, and do intend making Mead and a few more re-
> member me. I hope His Excellency will take me into his clemency,
> which will prevent me committing any more crime. I am your most
> obedient servant, James Lilly.

The *Inquirer's* comments were caustic: 'This is the most coolly impertinent letter we have ever received. This scamp presumes to dictate terms and to threaten. That this man should be at large to pen such an epistle is a reproach to the police authorities.'

The police authorities were not long in rising to this challenge. The very next day Mr S. S. Parker reported at York that he had seen Lilly on the York Road 24 kilometres towards Guildford. Although this automatically gave Lilly a 48-kilometre start, Mr L. J. Bayley, the government resident, volunteered to accompany personally Regan and a native assistant in pursuit.[28]

Lilly arrived at Horton's Inn at 'The Lakes' (Manaring Lake) about 3.00 pm. Mr and Mrs Horton were the only persons there when he entered, revolver in hand. Obviously referring to a boast of Horton's that had come to his ears, Lilly asked him if he had the double-barrelled gun he had threatened to shoot him with.

'If so', he said, 'you can have shot for shot now.'

Horton declined the invitation and plied Lilly with drink. He managed to keep him at the inn all that afternoon in the company of some of Mr Hamersley's men who arrived later. He stopped up until midnight with Lilly and the others, then left the bushranger in the kitchen with some ale and porter to keep him there. Bayley, Regan and Native Assistant Tommy arrived a few hours later, finding Lilly fast asleep. When Regan caught hold of him Lilly tried to bite him and draw his revolver, but after a brief scuffle he was secured with handcuffs. His revolver was found to be unloaded.[29]

Lilly was sentenced to twelve months' imprisonment and 100 lashes for unlawfully absconding from his appointed place of residence on the Canning River.[30] About a month later Frank Hall, who had not been seen since his escape, surrendered to the Vasse authorities. Ironically there were no officers on duty at the time and he was asked to wait while the sergeant was summoned and the keys to the lockup fetched.[31] He was sentenced to fifteen years' imprisonment.[32] Nevertheless as the son of a highly-respected settler he soon gained the trust of H. M. Lefroy, the superintendent of the Convict Establishment. Because of his 'well known bush experience and familiarity with the natives, and his general cleverness and smartness' Lefroy would choose him in 1863 as a companion on a particularly successful exploring expedition to the eastwards of York.[33] No doubt this earned Hall a well-deserved remission.

Early in 1861 Wheeler let his licence of the inn at Bailup lapse, yet although no accommodation was then available for travellers on the road, thirsty locals did not go dry. An unsavoury type named John McDonald set himself up there dispensing sly grog. It was a wild period in the inn's history. 'Disgraceful scenes of drunkenness' were reported by Resident Magistrate Harris of Toodyay,[34] and it is difficult to imagine Joe missing out on this riotous spree. In consequence one of the first official tasks of Alfred Durlacher, who took over as resident magistrate at Toodyay from Harris in April, was to obtain a Publicans' General Licence for the place for Messrs Albert and Barker, experienced and respectable men, who could be counted on to run the place properly.[35] The sly grog problem there was solved permanently in May, when John McDonald was committed for theft.[36] The good times were over.

REFERENCES

1. *Perth Gazette* 6 May 1853.
2. *Inquirer* 11 May 1853.
3. *Perth Gazette* 8 April, 10 June 1853.
4. *Inquirer* 18 May 1853.
5. *Perth Gazette* 13 May 1853.
6. Ibid 17 June 1853.
7. Ibid 13 May 1853.
8. *Inquirer* 18 May 1853; *Perth Gazette* 1 July 1853.
9. *Perth Gazette* 20 May 1853.
10. Convict Records, WAA Acc. No. 1156 R21B.
11. Police Records, WAA Acc. No. 129 2/236.
12. *Government Gazettes:* yearly lists of Publicans' Licences.
13. Police Records, WAA Acc. No. 129 (report dated 8 Nov. 1860).
14. *Government Gazettes:* yearly lists of Publicans' Licences.
15. Resident Magistrate of Newcastle to Colonial Secretary, 11, 12 August 1861, WAA CS0487, pp. 103-6.
16. *Inquirer* 7 November 1860.
17. Rica Erickson, *Old Toodyay and Newcastle* (Perth: Toodyay Shire Council 1974), pp. 107, 108.
18. *Inquirer* 7 November 1860.
19. Ibid 10 October 1860.
20. Ibid 7 November 1860.
21. Police Records, WAA Acc. No. 129 2/655.

22. *Inquirer* 7 November 1860.
23. Police Records, WAA Acc. No. 129 2/655.
24. Ibid.
25. Ibid.
26. Ibid.
27. Ibid 2/745.
28. Ibid 2/655.
29. Ibid 2/745.
30. *Inquirer* 5 December 1860.
31. Ibid 26 December 1860.
32. Ibid 23 January 1861.
33. Exploration Diaries, vol. 5, pp. 210, 213, 214.
34. Res. Mag. Newcastle to Col. Sec., January 1861, WAA CS0487.
35. Ibid 9 April 1861, p. 66.
36. Ibid 1 May 1861, p. 73.

Chapter three

August-October 1861

Early in August 1861 Joe caught a fine half-bred stallion which was unbranded. At Moondyne, in the presence of Thomas Cook and his son, he branded this horse on the offside of the neck with his own brand,[1] an unregistered but apparently recognized mark.[2] This was a crime virtually amounting to theft, and Joe must have been aware of that fact. Any cleanskin horse of breeding caught in the bush had to be reported and advertised. The Newcastle police soon came to hear of Joe's acquisition, and while riding the horse at Bailup on Tuesday morning 6 August, he was arrested by Police Sergeant John Kelly and Mounted Constable Robert Keane. Charged with horse stealing,[3] he was taken, with the horse as evidence, before Resident Magistrate Durlacher who, after due deliberation, adjourned the case to await further evidence.[4] Joe was secured in the lockup, while Constable Keane and his native assistant, the latter mounted on Mr Durlacher's horse since Sergeant Kelly had proceeded to Perth on the only other available police horse, were sent to search Joe's huts at Moondyne for other unbranded horses.[5]

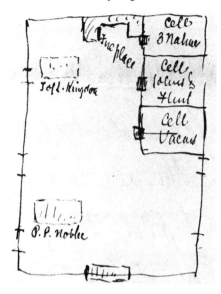

6 Sketch of the original Toodyay lockup by A. Durlacher

At this time the Toodyay lockup consisted of three cells within
the local convict depot. Its insecurity had been commented on by
Durlacher, but it was to be another four years before a new lock-up
would be constructed at Newcastle. The warder in charge of the
depot was John Jones, but the lockup inside was under the charge of
Thomas Burnside, a police constable and clerk to Durlacher.[6] At
6.30 pm on the Friday following Joe's arrest, these two secured the
lockup and depot. Inside the lockup were three Aboriginal prisoners
in one cell, and Joe and a ticket-of-leave holder named Robert
Flint, who was charged with bullock stealing, in another. The third
cell was left vacant for casual cases. Outside the cells, but locked
within the depot were ticket-of-leave holder Henry Kingston and a
probation prisoner named Noble. Outside in the stable was chained
the horse Joe was accused of stealing. A brand-new saddle and
bridle hung from the wall of the stable. Twelve hours later Burnside
was reporting the disappearance of Joe, horse, saddle and bridle to
Durlacher,[7] who carried out a hurried inspection of the depot,[8] and
then dashed off an irate letter to the colonial secretary.[9]

My Dear Sir,

The blackguard Johns has escaped during the night taking a horse (½ bred Entire) and my saddle and bridle (new). He broke out of the Cell and the Depot. Now perhaps my representations as to the Lockup will be believed.

Yours faithfully,
A. Durlacher

Subsequent investigations by Burnside revealed that the screws holding the catches of the locks and bolts of the cell door were out, either unscrewed from the outside or violently forced from the inside. Certainly the depot door appeared to have been forced from the inside as the box of the lock was broken. The chain holding the horse had been filed through, and the horse's tracks could be seen going along the road towards Guildford. None of the Newcastle police or horses were available to give chase to the escapee, so Durlacher instructed Constable Charles Wisbey, in from Northam, to ride to Guildford and report the matter, keeping his eyes open on the way.

With Wisbey gone, he proceeded to question the other prisoners, Flint and the two men who had slept in the depot. He came to the conclusion that Flint had known of Joe's intention to escape and remarked upon his own intention to 'deal with him after the case of Bullock Stealing against him [was] settled'.[10] His questioning exonerated Noble, but Durlacher reported:

With regard to T. of L. holder Kingston altho I have made a prisoner of him there is some difficulty in his case. Johns effected his escape either by loosening the screws during the day with an old knife (since found), or Kingston let him out. Flint states Kingston was up when Johns escaped, Kingston denies it . . . Flint is a consummate liar and may try to throw the blame on Kingston to save himself. The most suspicious circumstances with regard to Kingston is that when the Lockup Keeper examined as to how the escape was made Kingston picked up the knife in question and said, "Easy enough it is to unscrew these bolts", and immediately turned a screw with the knife in one of the other Cell doors. Now how could Kingston know the screws would turn so easily in the fastenings if he had not previously tried, or seen someone else try?[11]

Poor Kingston. Because of Durlacher's suspicion he forfeited his ticket of leave and was committed to the Convict Establishment to await the governor's pleasure.[12]

In the meantime, at 5.30 pm on the Saturday Constable Keane returned to Newcastle police station and was informed of Joe's escape. Early the next morning he and his native assistant set out towards Bailup and succeeded in capturing Joe at one of the sawyer's huts. No details have survived but later events show that there was no sign of the horse, saddle or bridle when the arrest was made. Joe was returned to the lockup, where presumably, repairs to the door fastenings had been made. Keane returned immediately to the bush to search for the missing horse.[13]

Joe was now charged with four more crimes: prison breaking, stealing a piece of chain, the property of Her Majesty (the piece attached to the horse), stealing a horse out of the police stable, stealing a bridle and saddle, the property of A. Durlacher Esquire, as well as the original charge of stealing a horse from some person or persons unknown.[14] Quite a list but, since none of the items he was accused of stealing had been found, it was impossible for Durlacher to commit him to trial at the quarter sessions of the Supreme Court for any except the charge of prison breaking.

It is interesting to compare this with the way Flint's case was handled. Flint was charged with stealing a bullock, but the skin was never found, nor anyone who could swear to the brand upon it. Durlacher stated that he 'did not feel justified in committing him for trial when he would be *acquitted on several legal points*' [author's italics]. As a ticket-of-leave man Flint was dealt with summarily by Durlacher himself who sentenced him to three years' penal servitude.[15] Being a free man, Joe could not be dealt with quite so easily.

The obvious insecurity of the lockup had led Durlacher to have it guarded by a constable during the day and he had ordered Burnside and a constable to sleep there at night,[16] so the transfer of Joe to the Perth lockup on 21 August was no doubt a great relief. In the meantime Keane had spared no effort to find the horse. In fact he and his native assistant had brought their horses to a state of near exhaustion in searching the bush. Sergeant Kelly had been unable to assist them, having been detained in Newcastle to deal with a murder case.[17] Finally on 28 August, Kelly, Keane and Native Assistant Jack proceeded to the bush in search of the horse. Sergeant Kelly's report to the superintendent of police tells the story [*verbatim et litteratim*]:

> I went to a natives' camp which was at some distance off. I enquired of them whether they had seen the tracks of a shod horse anywhere in the bush. One of them said yess. I called him away from the camp to a little distance. I told him I would give him a pound if he would show me the tracks and help me and my native to track the horse up until we found the horse dead or alive.
>
> He has done so and put me on the right tracks. 8 am on the morning of the 29th we all followed up the tracks and found that he went quite close to the Sawyers hut where P.C. Keane arrested Johns. On the following day I still followed the tracks up the hill and found the chain and handcuff that tied the stolen horse when in the police stable. We also found that he had taken the shoes off the horse at the same place.
>
> The natives and me still stuck to the tracks for about 8 or 9 miles further when I seen the horse at some distance lying on the ground. I galloped up and found that he was dead. I examined him and found that he has been shot with a ball through the forhead, and the head cut off the neck, both ears cut off and the offside of the neck where Johns had put his brand on was skined off, carried away and destroyed.
>
> I sent in a report of the same to the R.M. and requested that he would send T. Cook junior and T. Cook senior to identify the horse as being the same horse that Johns took out of the bush and branded at their station at Mondine. They both swear that he is the self same horse. P.C. Keane and myself can clearly prove that he is the same horse that I seized from Johns at Baylup on the morning of the 6th of August when I first arrested Johns in the presence of the Inspector.
>
> I have also found the R.Ms. bridle and saddle about 250 yards from where the horse is dead. After the horse being identified by the Cooks and self I returned to Station at 2 pm 31st, with the horses head, tail, hooves also the R.Ms. bridle and saddle, chain etc.[18]

The horse was found about 6 kilometres north-west of Bailup. The return of the sergeant and his gory trophies to Newcastle was the signal for Durlacher to pen an urgent request to the colonial secretary that Joe be brought to Newcastle to stand trial on the additional charges against him. He suggested that no stop should be made at

Bailup, and that more than one constable would be required to guard Joe: 'as he will certainly escape if he can and if he escapes, he will give great trouble as he is a thorough bushman and a most daring vagabond.'[19] Whether Joe was ever sent to Newcastle at this time is uncertain, but if he was, he received no sentence for any of the other charges.

He stood trial for breaking prison at the Supreme Court, Perth on Wednesday 2 October 1861. The case was presided over by His Honour Chief Justice Burt. A detailed report was given in the *Inquirer* the following week.

> Regina v Joseph Johns — The prisoner was charged with stealing a horse, the property of some person unknown, also with branding and taking a horse, the property of Her Majesty, and also with breaking prison when in custody at Toodyay.
>
> The Prisoner, who was defended by Mr. Landor, was tried for prison breaking only.
>
> Thomas Burnside, policeman and keeper of the Toodyay lock-up, also clerk to the Magistrate in that District, testified to the fact that the prisoner was in his custody, on remand on a charge of horse stealing, from the 6th to the 9th of August, and on the night of the latter day he was locked in his cell, the cells of the lockup being within the depot building.
>
> During the night he made his escape. On the morning of the 10th it was discovered that the lock of the cell and the door of the depot had been forced open. The witness considered that it was possible the lock could have been forced from the inside, although when he gave evidence before the Magistrates he had taken a different view of the matter. On cross examination he stated that, to try whether this could be done, he locked a person in the cell, who forced the lock and came out in his presence.
>
> On re-examination, he said that he did not observe any pieces of wood in the screw holes, but they had been made large.
>
> John Jones, a warder, stated that he was present when Burnside locked the prisoner in on the 9th, and saw him pull the fastenings to ascertain whether they were secure, and if anything had been loose at the time it would have been discovered. Locked the outer door at 7 o-clock, and gave the key to Burnside; that lock was then secure. Went next morning with Burnside and found the locks of both doors had been forced.
>
> On cross examination he gave it as his decided opinion that Johns

could not have escaped if he had not been let out by some body
outside; and on re-examination he said that the lock could not have
been forced from the inside. If the screws had been unloosened
during the day, the lock might have been forced from the inside
during the night, but this was not the case as Burnside, when locking
up the prisoner tried it, and found everything secure.

Robert Flint, a prisoner, was called by the Crown, but was not
examined by the Attorney General. In answer to a question from Mr.
Landor, said that he had been in the depot all day, and that no-one
could have loosened the screws of the lock without his being aware of it.

Mr. Landor in defence contended that it had not been proved that
the prisoner broke open the prison door, although there was no
doubt of his escape. He was not charged with escape but with prison-
breaking. He said that from the evidence it was clear that the lock
could not have been forced from the inside, and that the fastenings
outside were not tampered with by prisoner, because they were secure
when he was locked up for the night. The deed was done during the
night by someone who was outside, and who ought to be indicted
instead of the prisoner. He considered that the case for the prisoner
had been proved by the prosecutor, and the jury could not do otherwise than return a verdict of not guilty.

Upon the Attorney General rising to reply, Mr. Landor protested
against his so doing, when no witnesses were called, as he merely
represented the defunct Grand Jury, and did not prosecute upon an
ex-officio information.

This objection being overruled by the Court, the Attorney General,
in reply to Mr. Landor contended that the Crown was not obliged to
prove that the prisoner actually broke the fastenings, it being quite
sufficient to prove that it was done with his privity and concurrence.
It was possible the lock might have been broke with out his knowledge, and there was no positive evidence that he was privy to it
being done, but then there was the fact of his escape, which was
something to show that he was a party concerned.

The Chief Justice, in addressing the jury, stated that the fact of the
prisoner's escape was not conclusive evidence that he broke prison,
and to prove this latter it was not necessary to produce evidence that
he actually broke out of prison, but it would be enough if there was
sufficient presumption that the act was done with his connivance. It
was for the jury to judge whether there was sufficient presumption of
the guilt of the prisoner in this instance and was their duty to give
him the benefit of any reasonable doubt.

We will never know for sure whether Joe managed this escape on his own or with outside help as suggested by Mr Landor. However the latter seems unlikely. After all, if his friends wished to help him, all they had to do was to steal the horse, destroy it and burn the hide. Lack of evidence would then have acquitted him. Certainly Joe's friends at the sawyers' camp assisted by supplying him with a gun to shoot the horse and were no doubt fitting Joe out for an extended sojourn in the bush when Keane caught up with him, but it is doubtful that they had any part in the actual escape. Durlacher's suspicions of Kingston might have had some foundation, but it is difficult to imagine Kingston risking his ticket of leave to assist in such a hair-brained scheme. At any rate, whoever broke the locks, the jury had no doubts that it was done with Joe's knowledge and their verdict was guilty. Chief Justice Burt pronounced the sentence: three years' penal servitude.

REFERENCES

1. Police Records, WAA Acc. No. 129 3/891.
2. *Government Gazettes:* lists of registered stock brands from 1853 to 1861
3. Police Records, WAA Acc. No. 129 3/891.
4. Magistrate's Report dated 6 August 1861, WAA CS0487, p. 201.
5. Resident Magistrate of Newcastle to Colonial Secretary, 11, 12 Augus 1861, WAA CS0487, pp. 103-6.
6. *Inquirer* 9 October 1861.
7. Res. Mag. Newcastle to Col. Sec., 11, 12 August 1861, WAA CS0487 pp. 103-6.
8. Convict Records, WAA Acc. No. 1156 OCC2.
9. Res. Mag. Newcastle to Col. Sec., 10 August 1861, WAA CS0487, p. 102
10. Ibid 11, 12 August 1861, pp. 103-6.
11. Ibid.
12. Ibid 14 August 1861, p. 108.
13. Ibid 11, 12 August 1861, pp. 103-6.
14. Police Records, WAA Acc. No. 129 3/812.
15. Res. Mag. Newcastle to Col. Sec., 21 August 1861, WAA CS0487, p. 113
16. Ibid 19 August 1861, p. 112.
17. Police Records, WAA Acc. No. 129 3/812.
18. Ibid 3/891.
19. Res. Mag. Newcastle to Col. Sec., 31 August 1861, WAA CS0487, p. 117

Chapter four

1861-1864

Joe was transferred to the Convict Establishment at Fremantle as colonial convict number 5889. His possessions, which were confiscated and sold, amounted to a blue slop, a flannel shirt, a pair of fustian trousers, a pair of boots, a felt hat and a small tooth comb. These fetched the sum of 3s. 2d.[1] They were replaced by trousers, waistcoat and jacket made of white duck (canvas) and stamped with black broad arrows, the summer convict uniform. In winter a heavier, dark-grey or brown fustian suit, also stamped with the distinctive broad arrows, was issued.

From this time on Joe's life was regulated by the strict prison routine. He awoke to the first bell at 5.00 am, folded his bedding and awaited the unlocking of his cell door so that he could attend the morning roll-call. After that there was just time for a quick wash before parading for one of the several work details, either inside or outside the prison walls. At 8.00 am, after two hours' work, the prisoners were marched to the mess hall for breakfast and morning prayers, then back to work at 9.00 am. The midday break

was taken between 12.00 noon and 1.30 pm, then the prisoners
were returned to their respective tasks until supper-time at 6.00 pm.
Between supper and evening prayers at 7.30 pm the men were
allowed to move about in the exercise yard. Smoking was allowed
there, but not inside the barracks or on the works. As a reconvicted
prisoner, Joe was not allowed the normal tobacco ration, and if he
smoked, he would have had to cadge both pipe and tobacco from
his fellow-inmates. After evening prayers the men were returned to
their cells and the lights were turned out at 8.00 pm. The days were
made more dreary by the diet. Under the 1849 regulations each
prisoner had to be given 'a sufficient quantity of plain and wholesome food'. This was construed by the authorities as a monotonous
round of bread, meat, potatoes and tea, with occasional additions
of soup, rice or biscuits, but at least it was sufficient.

While Joe was settling down to prison life once more, James
Everett was in all kinds of trouble at Newcastle. Cocky and confident, in September he advertised four horses caught on his run, two
of which he intended to sell if no claimant came forward. He also
inserted a challenge in the *Perth Gazette* 'to trot a pony under 14
hands against anything that [could] be produced in the district'.[2]

The event was to take place at the Toodyay Fair, but before then
Everett was taken before Resident Magistrate Durlacher on four
counts of selling spirits without a licence. It seems that Everett had
sued a debtor on a promissory note of £10, and in revenge the
debtor had informed the police of Everett's sly grog sales.[3] The
Queen's Head and other hotels in Toodyay had been closed when
the new townsite of Newcastle had been declared and Everett was
then unlicensed. He was found guilty on three charges and fined a
total of £120,[4] no small amount in those days. But still worse was to
follow. Everett accused a man named Esau Wetherall of stealing
and killing an ox of his and Wetherall was committed for trial.
Out on bail, Wetherall promptly accused Everett of horse stealing.
Everett was arrested by Sergeant Kelly and thrown into the Royal
Engineer's Store at Newcastle,[5] the Toodyay lockup evidently being
considered too insecure to hold him.

The authorities went to incredible lengths to ensure a conviction
for Everett. When his solicitor arrived in Newcastle he found both
the crown solicitor and the superintendent of police assisting Dur-

lacher 'to get up a grand case'.[6] The hearing was held behind closed doors, an unusual step, and the only witnesses called were said to be Wetherall and Joseph Johns. Convict records show only that Joe had been transferred temporarily to the custody of the Perth police and there is no record of his being sent to Newcastle for this hearing. Nevertheless Everett's solicitor, Mr Howell, stated quite definitely that he was present and there is little doubt that Joe would have had some knowledge of the affair. Everett was committed for trial at the Supreme Court. Mr Howell experienced much difficulty in the matter of bail for his client, as the crown solicitor was firmly opposed to the very idea, and it was only after much argument that bail was eventually set at all. The amount required was a staggering £2000 of which Everett was able to raise only half. Duncan McPherson and a man named O'Neil, friends in need, stood surety for the remainder.[7]

On bail in December, Everett acquired Avon Locations 300 and 319. The latter surrounded Julimar Spring and one of Joe's strongly built horse traps. Everett would continue this policy of buying up small blocks containing similar springs and traps for several years. It is possible that a certain amount of malice was attached to this course of action, and it is not hard to imagine the trend of Joe's thoughts on the matter when he returned to the district and found all his traps in private property.

The Supreme Court trials of both Everett and Wetherall were farcical. In Everett's case neither of the witnesses present at the magistrate's hearing at Newcastle (Wetherall and Joe) were called by the crown prosecutor and the defence proved that the horse he was accused of stealing was actually his own. Wetherall's case was similar, and in the end both were acquitted.[8]

In March 1862, after serving seven months, Joe was transferred from Fremantle to Perth where he worked in a convict party for fifteen months.[9] Sailing craft and several small steamers regularly plied between the colony's port and its capital, but Joe probably made the journey in a police cart, either crossing the Swan by ferry at Fremantle (there being no bridge there at that time), or following the road south of the river over Canning Bridge and the Perth Causeway. Constituted as a city in 1856, Perth still retained the appearance of a rural township. Few of the buildings lining its

neatly laid out streets exceeded two stories and most town houses
had extensive orchards. Joe was housed in the Perth gaol which had
been handed over to the Imperial Establishment some years earlier.
Most convicts stationed there at this time were employed on the
construction of an imposing new residence for the governor, where
Joe's woodworking ability was no doubt put to good use. Apparently
he behaved well, but others were not so content with their lot, so
that escapes and bushranging became rife during this period.

On a stormy night in July 1862 two teamsters were attacked at
Greenmount by five convicts of the road party stationed there.
Cheeses and other goods, as well as money, were stolen, and when
caught soon after, the men were charged with robbery with violence,
then a capital offence. One man turned Queen's evidence but the
other four were sentenced to be hanged. This was said to be the
first offence of that kind committed in the colony and the men had
no idea of the punishment prescribed for their crime, expecting no
more than a few months prison if caught. Eventually two were
reprieved because they did not appear to have actually used violence,
but the remaining two were only saved from the gallows at the last
minute by a meeting of the Executive Council which reviewed the
case in the light of petitions sent in to the governor.[10]

Later in the month two men escaped from Fremantle and one
from the Guildford depot. The former were taken at Mr Middleton's
place on the Canning River and the latter near York. Another
convict made his escape from the Perth work party, but was recaptured almost immediately.[11]

Disturbed at the frequency of these escapes, the York Agricultural
Society requested that some protection be afforded to travellers by
locating a police outpost near Horton's inn at 'The Lakes' (Manaring
Lake). This request was agreed to by the governor and police stations
were subsequently established both there and at Bailup on the Toodyay road.[12]

In August a bushranger named John Gray escaped from the York
gaol. He had committed many depredations in various districts, until
he had been captured at Mahogany Creek by Sergeant Piesse and
lodged in the York gaol again. The gaoler, Mills, was considered
responsible for the escape and dismissed from his post. Gray remained
at large for nearly a fortnight, although a reward of £20 was offered

for his apprehension. He acquired a double-barrelled gun from somewhere along the York road, and when the police eventually caught up with him, he threatened to shoot the native tracker who was in the lead. Fortunately for the tracker, the constable caught up and yelled at Gray to drop the gun. Gray did as he was instructed and was escorted back to prison.[13] In the meantime two probation men from a road party had absconded and were robbing travellers on the Northam road.[14]

Later in the same month James Lilly managed to give his warders the slip while working in a quarry near Fremantle. At the time he was garbed in a recently adopted uniform for difficult prisoners. This consisted of brown clothing with red stripes, a broad arrow and the letters SDC (Stringent Discipline Class) added. Lilly threw off these conspicuous clothes and, wearing only his shirt and boots, ran to a nearby hut, where he acquired a new wardrobe. From his prior record it was thought that the police would have trouble in catching him, but to everybody's relief he gave himself up voluntarily at Pinjarra only a week after his escape.[15]

One night in October a prisoner named John Williams made his escape from Fremantle. Williams was an audacious fellow who had broken out of the Busselton gaol only a few months earlier. Before leaving Fremantle he committed a robbery at the prison superintendent's house, then stole the convict surgeon's horse. The police caught up with him at the Murray River, but a tracker who swam the river to take him came off second best in the struggle and Williams took possession of his revolver. He committed robberies at Pinjarra and Australind, then acquired a boat at the latter place, and rowed some distance along the Leschenault Estuary. At Busselton, he succeeded in getting away from the colony in an American whaler.[16]

In January of 1863 there were several escapes made from the Mount Eliza quarry party. Two of these absconders headed up the Canning River, stealing clothing and a gun and ammunition from settlers' houses on the way. When police caught up with them they threatened to shoot the first that touched them. However the police had three guns to their one and, after some thought, they surrendered. The gun they had stolen was found to be loaded with a charge about 10 centimetres in depth, which could well have blown their heads off had they pulled the trigger. They were sentenced to four years in irons. Another Mount Eliza runaway headed north past the Benedictine Mission (Subiaco), using a novel method to fool police trackers: whenever he reached a fence he walked along the lower rail. In spite of this he was soon recaptured.[17]

In early April five prisoners escaped from the Convict Establishment but they were quickly caught.[18] A few weeks later another three escaped from the construction works at the new Fremantle Asylum, and though they managed to get into the Darling Range east of Kelmscott, they were eventually hunted down and returned to prison.[19]

So far, although the police had been kept busy, very little violence had accompanied these escapes. Then on 16 June 1863 the colony was shocked by the brutal battering of an elderly man at Joseph Hardey's Peninsula Farm near Perth. A convict named John Thomas had succeeded in escaping from a road party the previous day, taking with him a blanket, a small axe and a dinner knife. He was tracked to Guildford, where it was found he had crossed the river on the ferry and headed towards Hardey's. On his arrival there, Thomas broke into a worker's hut to get food and clothing, but was surprised in the act by the owner, an old man named Duncan Urquhart. Soon afterwards Urquhart was found by Hardey: the old man was still alive; his head had been bashed in with the axe, which lay in the hut, together with a prison jacket bearing the number 7279, Thomas's convict number. An intensive manhunt was organized, and Thomas, wearing Urquhart's clothes, was captured two days later by Police Constable Michael Lally near Lloyds' '19 Mile Inn' on the York road. Lally marched his prisoner to Mahogany Creek where he decided to put up for the night at the Prince of Wales Inn. After a meal Lally escorted his prisoner to their room, secured him with handcuffs and threw himself onto the bed. Lally had been following Thomas up without rest for three days and was now so overcome with fatigue that he soon fell asleep. This gave his prisoner, who was said to have had unusually small hands and wrists, the opportunity to slip his handcuffs and escape. One can imagine poor Lally's feelings when he awoke the following morning. However, he was exonerated of any blame in the affair. Thomas was recaptured two days later by Mr McDermott at Upper Swan and marched into Guildford, where he was handed back to the police.[20]

Old Duncan Urquhart hovered between life and death in the Colonial Hospital for two and a half months and finally succumbed to his extensive injuries on 24 August. Thomas was charged with the murder and went on trial the following month. He claimed self-defence but was found guilty and sentenced to death.

In January 1864 a notorious character named Mercer managed to get away from Fremantle. He headed for the Albany road but was caught near Thomas Saw's Narrogin Inn, not far past Kelmscott. While being handcuffed, he twisted out of the constable's grasp and made for the bush. Although called upon to stop, he refused and left the constable no choice but to fire. As the *Perth Gazette* so quaintly put it, the 'ball sent after him took effect in his leg, and his further progress was thus checked.' Mercer was returned to Fremantle and placed in the convict hospital.[21]

During February a convict named Johnson bolted from the Seven Mile Gully road party near York. He was joined by McKeen and Rose, absconders from the Yangedine road party, and the three headed eastwards. They robbed Mr Robert Hardey's shepherd, then travelled to 'Cubbin', where they stuck up Mr Woodly with his own guns. On 26 February they visited Mr E. Parker's station near Mount Stirling, where they held up the hutkeeper and stole enough supplies for an extended stay in the bush. They also seized a native girl as a guide, tying her legs each night so that she could not run away.

They were finally captured about 130 kilometres east of York by Police Constables Edwards and Sullivan and their two native assistants. Johnson was alone when the police came up. He attempted to make a run for it, then, seeing that escape was impossible he turned and aimed his gun at Sullivan who fired instantly, wounding Johnson slightly in the neck. Johnson surrendered immediately and was secured with chains. His two companions were discovered at a spring about a kilometre away. McKeen seized his double-barrelled gun but put it down at Sullivan's request. They were brought back to York in chains.[22]

In the meantime a violin-playing charmer named William Graham had embarked on a career of bushranging. Although a ticket-of-leave man, Graham was allowed to carry a gun as he was employed collecting birds for the natural history collection of Reverend G. Bostock. He had been employed by Mr Quartermaine of 'Yewenup' near Beverley for about eighteen months but had left the previous September. During his stay at Quartermaine's he had, in the parlance of those days, 'usurped Quartermaine's place in the establishment'. Quartermaine, returning home unexpectedly one night, tapped on his bedroom window for admittance. He was answered by a shotgun blast through the glass which hit him in the chest and knocked him down. The shot was followed closely by Graham who took to his heels. He arrived at Mr Randell's place in York early the next morning and demanded his horse which Randell was minding. When asked what the hurry was he replied that he had been caught in bed with mother Quartermaine, had fired through the window and did not know whether he had killed the old man or not.

Quartermaine had survived and the matter was soon reported to the police who instigated an intensive manhunt. Graham, however, proved to be an elusive quarry. On March 14 he returned to Quartermaine's, stole supplies and ammunition and left a note for Mrs Quartermaine. He then headed south visiting several outlying homesteads to the east of Kojonup, including Norrish's place at Ettakup, Treasure's at Martinup and Drolf's at 'Malgatup'. At all these places he made no secret of his intention to shoot any police who approached him. He carried a double-barrelled gun, one barrel loaded with shot for ordinary use and the other with ball for emergencies. Police trackers found that he invariably rode in the bush alongside roads, usually keeping the road within the range of his gun. The police in pursuit adopted the measure of sending their native on ahead in the centre of the road as a decoy, while they rode in the bush at either side. Graham was eventually captured at the Fitzgerald River by Sergeant Finlay and a party of police and trackers who shared a reward of £16 10s. Finlay was commended for his diplomacy in persuading Graham to surrender.[23]

While the hue and cry after Graham was at its height, two prisoners were discovered hiding in the yard of the Convict Establishment, obviously intending to go over the wall at nightfall. On the previous day a mass escape of ten prisoners had taken place at North Fremantle, where work had begun on the construction of a bridge across the Swan. The sentries fired after the fugitives, and

although only one was hit, two surrendered immediately; three more
were captured that same evening. Another three were returned to
the Convict Establishment within the next few days but the pursuit
after the remaining two, Bernard Woottan and Charles Lossom,
was protracted and arduous. Woottan, one of three who had escaped
ten months previously and spent some time bushranging on the
Canning, was now determined to remain at large. He and Lossom
were reported to have held up settlers and shepherds as far apart as
Beverley and Harvey, and in April were responsible for a number of
robberies near Bunbury and Busselton. They were finally captured
by Sergeant Dyer and a party of police and trackers in the Blackwood River district.[24] For absconding and resisting lawful apprehension each received 100 lashes. The cat-o'-nine-tails used to administer
this punishment was similar in weight and size to those used on
board British warships.

Early in March the schooner *New Perseverance* sailed from Fremantle bearing an exploration party bound for the Glenelg River in
the North-West. One of the party was a convict named Henry
Wildman who had informed the prison authorities that in 1856, as
first mate of a Dutch ship disabled near Camden Harbour he had
gone ashore and found eight nuggets of gold. These were supposed
to have been sold to a bullion dealer in Liverpool for £416. Great
excitement was aroused by this story and, when Wildman offered to
lead an expedition to the spot in return for a remission of the twelve
years remaining of his fifteen years' term, the government contributed
£150 towards expenses and Police Inspector F. K. Panter was appointed leader of the expedition. On arriving at the Glenelg River,
Wildman either would not, or more likely, could not show them the
place. The expedition nevertheless was not a complete failure. Panter
estimated that the discovery of vast areas of good pastoral land had
cost only 'one-fourteenth part of a farthing per acre'. Unfortunately
the expedition's glowing reports ultimately resulted in the ill-fated
attempt at settlement at Roebuck Bay, where Panter and others
were later massacred by natives. Whether Wildman had ideas of
escape is unknown, though he certainly succeeded in obtaining a
pleasant holiday from the Convict Establishment. When the expedition returned to Fremantle he was employed on the chain-gang at
the Fremantle Bridge. He did not receive a certificate of freedom

until 1874, yet there is no evidence that he headed north and became rich after his release, so his story about the nuggets may be disregarded.[25]

At 1.00 am on the morning of March 30 two prisoners stole away from the Point Resolution convict party but were found on the afternoon of the same day hiding in a clump of rushes in Mr Gallop's garden at Dalkeith. One of these would-be bushrangers was named Edward Kelly, but he was apparently unrelated to his then ten-year old namesake who would later make that name so infamous.[26]

Late in July William ('The Fiddler') Graham, serving a life term for the wounding of Mr Quartermaine, succeeded in escaping from the Convict Establishment. He and other stringent-discipline prisoners wearing unconnected leg irons were at work quarrying stone within the prison compound. They were watched by an armed sentry, who stood on a ledge of rock with his back to the wall, and an unarmed warder who supervised the work below. During the afternoon of Thursday July 28 an unchained prisoner who had occasion to walk between the sentry and the wall, suddenly seized the latter from behind. The sentry cried out and managed to let his musket tumble over the rock, but before the warder could reach it, the convicts took possession. Graham scrambled up the rock face and held the sentry while the other prisoners raced for a ladder which they threw against the wall. Graham, William Watkins and two others succeeded in scaling this, hurled themselves over the wall and scattered but they were all recaptured within minutes. Graham was tackled in a nearby garden by an off-duty pensioner named Barrett who sat on him until assistance arrived. All four participants in this futile attempt received 100 lashes.[27]

The worst trouble spot for the authorities was without doubt the Fremantle Bridge works. During the three years this bridge was under construction, repeated escape attempts were made by the convicts working there. No less than seven men absconded from there during September 1864 and a mass escape in the same month was only prevented by the quick thinking of Warder Hollis. So persistent were these attempts that the authorities were forced to take special precautions. The guard was strengthened, thick scrub surrounding the site was cleared away for a distance of 200 to 300 metres and a police station was established at North Fremantle, but still the escapes continued. Further measures included dividing the prisoners into two groups. Those in chains were invariably worked at the top of the embankment in full view of all the sentries. A flag-staff was mounted on a nearby rise overlooking the works with a man in constant attendance who would signal the Convict Establishment when trouble occurred. At the Convict Establishment a cannon was set up, near the guard-room, under the charge of an artillery-man told off for that special duty. Tests in October 1864, using a charge of powder weighing 3 pounds, were not heard in Perth but certainly gave a satisfactory warning to all police and off-duty pensioners in the vicinity of the works, rattling windows throughout Fremantle and smashing most of those in the guard-house.[28] The police posted at the North Fremantle station took the precaution of keeping two horses standing in the stables at all times, saddled, bridled and ready for immediate action.[29]

These precautions had the desired effect, for when Wildman and two others succeeded in escaping from the bridge works some months later, they were speedily captured by Constables Stack and Armstrong stationed at North Fremantle.[30] A later attempt by Bernard Woottan, William Watkins and a man named Smith is described by the Fremantle correspondent to the *Perth Gazette.*

> At 4.00 p.m. the signal gun at the Establishment boomed forth its warning, accompanied by the ringing of the bell, and quickly responded to by the shrill bugle call; the Police were not long in answering the signal, nor were the enrolled force slow in responding to the "assembly"; in a few minutes our streets were alive with pensioners "doubling", police galloping, and groups standing at every door. And what was it all about? The old cry again, prisoners escaped from the bridge party; the particulars as near as I can learn are as follows—
>
> Whilst the flat was upon the north side and during the temporary absence of the ferryman on this side, three prisoners after cutting the ferry rope unobserved, entered the small boat and glided quickly to the opposite shore without attracting attention, as they were supposed to be the regular ferrymen. After crossing and proceeding a few yards they met a lad carrying a gun which they wrested from his hands, and started off past the pensioner's cottages, followed by a number of boys and pensioners. The man stationed upon the lookout hill, seeing that something was wrong hoisted the signal flag, which

was soon answered by the alarm before mentioned. They were not long at liberty; the pensioners kept them in sight and were shortly joined by the police who, finding the ferry boat adrift, swam their horses across and assisted in capturing the men within a short distance of North Fremantle . . . The firing of the alarm gun again played sad havoc amongst the windows, from 18 to 24 having suffered from the concussion.[31]

While all these events were taking place, Joe had completed his sentence and enjoyed a brief period of freedom. He had been transferred from Perth to Fremantle on 25 June 1863, and less than a fortnight later was included in the North Fremantle work party. Rather than take part in the futile escapes attempted by other members of that detail, Joe voiced his dissatisfaction by petitioning for a ticket of leave. The petition was ignored but his continued good behaviour eventually earned him a remission of sentence and he was recalled to Fremantle on 2 February 1864. Three days later he was discharged to the Mount Eliza convict depot.[32] His signature on the receipt for the 3s 2d from the sale of his clothes is the only example of Joe's writing known to have survived.[33] Joe spent a further three days searching for work in Perth, at last finding employment as a charcoal burner for a man named George Vagg.[34] His ticket of leave was issued somewhat tardily two days later.[35] The job involved burning timber in pits, then digging out the resulting charcoal for which he was paid 6d per barrel. He stuck at this job until March when he hired himself out as a stockman for £1 a week. Towards the end of June 1864 he left Perth and apparently headed back to Newcastle, where his certificate of freedom was delivered in August.

7 Joe's signature

In the light of Joe's later behaviour, both in and out of prison, some explanation for this exemplary record appears necessary. It should be remembered that he had given no trouble whilst serving his original sentence, earning his conditional pardon after serving only six years of a ten years' sentence. His escape from the Toodyay lockup seems to have been effected mainly for the purpose of destroying the evidence against him, in which he succeeded. Without the branded horse, the charge of horse stealing was dropped and the authorities were left with only the much lesser charge of prison breaking. For horse stealing Joe could have been sentenced to ten or fifteen years, and there can be no doubt that he was reasonably content with his three years' sentence. He stayed out of trouble and was out on a ticket of leave after serving only two years four months, most of which had been spent outside the prison walls.

REFERENCES

1. Convict Records, WAA Acc. No. 1156 V14.
2. *Perth Gazette* 27 September 1861.
3. *Inquirer* 23 October 1861.
4. Resident Magistrate of Newcastle to Colonial Secretary, 14 October 1861, WAA CS0487, p. 126.
5. Ibid 19 Ocotber 1861, p. 129.
6. *Perth Gazette* 25 October 1861; *Inquirer* 8 January 1862.
7. *Inquirer* 30 October 1861.
8. Ibid 8 January 1862.
9. Convict Records, WAA Acc. No. 1156 R7.
10. *Inquirer* 9, 16, 23 July, 6, 13, 20 August 1862.
11. *Perth Gazette* 1 August 1862.
12. Ibid 8 August 1862.
13. *Inquirer* 6, 20 August 1862.
14. Ibid 20 August 1862.
15. *Inquirer* 27 August, 3 September 1862; *Perth Gazette* 29 August 1862.
16. *Inquirer* 27 August 1862; *Perth Gazette* 31 October, 7, 21, November, 5 December 1862, 27 July 1866.
17. *Perth Gazette* 16, 23 January 1863.
18. Ibid 10 April 1863.
19. Ibid 1 May 1863.
20. *Inquirer* 24 June 1863; *Perth Gazette* 19, 26 June, 21, 28 August, 4 September 1863.

21. *Perth Gazette* 29 January 1864.
22. *Inquirer* 2, 9, 16 March 1864.
23. Police Records, WAA Acc. No. 129 5/901, 5/966, 6/58; *Perth Gazette* 11, 25 March, 22, 29 April, 6, 20 May 1864.
24. Convict Records, WAA Acc. No. 1156 R&D4; *Inquirer* 16, 23 March 1864; *Perth Gazette* 18, 25 March, 1 April, 6 May 1864.
25. J. S. Battye, *Western Australia: A History*, pp. 264-7; Malcolm A. C. Fraser, *Western Australian Year Book 1902-04*, 13th edn (Perth: Government Printer 1906), p. 828; James Martin and Frederick Kennedy Panter, *Journals and Reports of Two Voyages to the Glenelg River and the North-West Coast of Australia 1863-4* (Perth: A. Shenton 1864), Panter's report p. 14; *Government Gazette* 8 December 1874, p. 238.
26. Convict Records, WAA Acc. No. 1156 R&D4; *Perth Gazette* 1 April 1864.
27. *West Australian Times* 4 August 1864; *Perth Gazette* 5 August 1864.
28. *Perth Gazette* 28 October 1864.
29. Ibid 14, 21 October 1864.
30. Ibid 23 June 1865.
31. Ibid 1 September 1865.
32. Convict Records, WAA Acc. No. 1156 R&D4.
33. Ibid V14.
34. Ibid R4.
35. Ibid R21B.

Chapter five

1864-1865

As a free man Joe's movements were no longer restricted, and in the latter part of 1864, apparently finding things hard at Newcastle, where the horse traps he had built had been taken over by others, he moved to Kelmscott on the Canning River. Kelmscott was then a tiny rural village, possessing little more than a church and police station which served the scattered farming population.

Joe was employed as a casual farm labourer by Henry Martin whose house was situated on the east bank of the Canning, not far from the street now bearing his name. It was the first house ever built in Kelmscott, and although long since demolished, its position is indicated by a stone cairn and marble inscription, erected by historically-minded locals. Martin took in cattle on his property and augmented his income by travelling about the colony repairing cart wheels. It was while Martin was away on such a trip to Newcastle, early in 1865, that trouble began brewing again for Joe.

In late January Edward Turner, who was also in the agistment business, set loose a steer belonging to William Wallace. The steer, which trotted happily off towards good grazing on the Canning, was an unusual animal, dark red with a white ring around his tail and peculiar deformed horns. He was branded A. M. upside down on the rump and aptly named 'Bright'.[1]

Just before leaving for Newcastle, Martin noticed Bright between his place and the Narrogin Inn. Although Martin's brand was a figure 2, the original Martin family brand had been A.M. conjoined. Bright had been born at Martin's place, his mother having been purchased from Wallace, who had taken the first calf in part payment. Martin killed a beast for meat before leaving for Newcastle, but he later denied emphatically the suggestion that this was Bright.[2]

During Martin's absence Joe spoke to a man named William Reid at the stockyards. He told Reid that Wallace's steer was dead and eaten, and that he had put something on Martin's premises that would 'lag him'.[3] When Martin returned home Reid informed him of what had been said and was able to lead him to a spot on the river bank just below the Martin's garden where Bright's skull was found in about 1.5 metre of water. Martin promptly went to the police.

On 28 March Constable Richard Buck called at Martin's, took statements and examined the skull. A further search revealed Bright's hide and tail buried near Martin's garden. Mrs Martin then recalled lending Joe a gun to shoot a squeaker (a small bird) while her husband was away. On the same day she had visited a friend nearby and both of them had heard a shot. Later she would say:

> On coming home from Mrs. McCormack's I met Johns coming out of my kitchen. I went to bed early that night. Johns slept in the house. I heard him walking about during the night. In the morning I asked him what made him so restless. He said the fleas troubled him. I found the gun resting against the fence. I asked Johns what sort of a beast Wallace's steer was. He smiled and said, very likely it was either killed or poisoned and I said what makes you say that Johns. He replied Buckingham's cattle had died and why shouldn't that die. I did not know then that the steer named "Bright" was dead.[4]

The following day Buck went to Palmer's place about 1 kilometre further up the river where Joe was then employed. Joe was arrested on a charge of killing an ox with felonious intent and conveyed to the Perth lockup. On the way he produced a note, supposedly written by Mrs Martin, instructing him to kill a beast to replace the one that went bad. He asked that it be handed to the police magistrate. Buck asked whether the note referred to the beast whose hide he had but Joe snapped, 'You want to know too much.'

The case was tried at the Supreme Court on 5 July 1865. Acting for the defence was Mr Howell who, it may be remembered, had successfully defended Everett on the horse stealing charge in 1862. If Joe hoped for a similar success he was sadly disappointed. Although the evidence was purely circumstantial, the jury returned a verdict of guilty after a retirement of only twenty minutes and he was sentenced to ten years' penal servitude.[5]

Joe was to protest his innocence of this charge for the rest of his life, and recalling his past good behaviour in prison and comparing it with his later determination not to serve this sentence, one does begin to doubt his guilt. After poring over the evidence still available, the author is inclined to the view that Joe did not kill Bright. There is little doubt that he was responsible for placing the incriminating evidence on Martin's property and he was probably well aware of the identity of the person who killed the beast, but, perhaps through a misplaced sense of honour, he refused to name him. Thus he deprived himself of his only means of defence after Mrs Martin had denied writing the note. Whatever the truth of the matter, Joe was convinced that his sentence was unjust and he entered prison in a far different frame of mind than when he had begun his previous sentence.

Registered as convict number 8189, Joe changed into convict garb once again. His possessions this time were listed as '1 Pair of Trousers, 1 Blue Serge Shirt, 1 Pair of Boots, 1 Strap and 1 Old Felt Hat'.[6] These fetched only 1s 6d at auction.[7]

Convict escapes were still taking place frequently. A few weeks earlier two men had absconded from a working party at Bunbury. One was captured about 130 kilometres east of York and informed the police that his companion was still further into the interior. The second man was eventually found about the same distance east of Kojonup, having travelled through previously unexplored country. As a contemporary newspaper put it, 'He received a reward of 2 years imprisonment from the Police Magistrate for his exploration.'[8]

Not long after Joe entered prison, an informer amongst the convicts gave the warders details of hiding places for tools to be used in
escape attempts. The authorities were astounded at the number
and variety of tools in these caches and questions were asked by the
governor himself.[9]

Some time after this, there was a determined attempt by six
convicts from the Geraldton depot to take possession of the coastal
vessel *Geraldton Lass*. They were only thwarted by O'Grady, the
master, who escaped and gave the alarm.[10]

In late October two absconders named Daniel Duffy and Mathew
Brooks were being harboured by Edward Johnston, a shoemaker of
Northam. Duffy and Brooks made several successful forays, robbing
the houses of outlying settlers, then returning to the shelter of Johnston's home. On the morning of Wednesday 1 November they stuck up
the house of George Christmas who was absent at the time. One man
stood guard over the occupants of the house while the other proceeded
to ransack the place. They stole money, guns, provisions and a quantity of brandy. The following morning they demanded breakfast at
Reynolds' place. They returned to Johnston's on Saturday night, tap-
ping at his bedroom window and asking his wife to send him into the
other room. There were already five lodgers in the other room and the
addition of Duffy, Brooks and Johnston made quite a crowd. The
stolen brandy was passed around and a prolonged drinking bout took
place. At about 3 am Mrs Johnston heard a shot and, on entering the
room, found her husband lying on the floor dead. Two of her lodgers
were sitting up bleary-eyed and the rest were still insensibly drunk. On
looking out the door she saw Duffy and Brooks running away. A
tremendous hue and cry was raised after these two later the same
morning, most of the young men of the district turning out to assist in
what the *Perth Gazette* was to call 'the apprehension of these desperate
villains'. The pair were captured that same afternoon by Sergeant
John Kelly in a deserted hut at the 'wash pool' near Mr Cook's. They
went on trial in January 1866 and both received the death sentence.[11]

During this period Joe had been careful not to disclose his rebel-
lious feelings to the prison authorities, and, his behaviour being
considered satisfactory, was included in a draft of prisoners discharged to the Canning work party on Wednesday 1 November.[12]
Also in that draft was a prisoner named David Evans.

Evans and his partner John James had been amongst 280 convicts who arrived on the *Racehorse* in August.[13] Both were sentenced to penal servitude for life and felt that they had nothing to lose by attempting to escape. The authorities had separated these two, sending James to the Mount Eliza depot and Evans to Barndon Hill, but Evans had teamed up with two other *Racehorse* convicts in a determined escape attempt. The attempt failed and all three were returned to the Convict Establishment, sentenced to an additional twelve months and sixty lashes.[14] Now, with his back fully healed, Evans was again in a position to attempt an escape. In fact his chances looked a great deal brighter now that he had met Joe.

Joe himself was jubilant that they had been included in the Canning Flats work party as he knew the area intimately and had friends living nearby. They spent only a week in the work party before slipping quietly away in the night. When their absence was discovered the warder was in a quandary. He realized that the escape should be promptly reported but he could not leave the rest of his prisoners unguarded. He chose one of the more trustworthy, a man named William Taylor, to alert the police and the superintendent of the Convict Establishment, for which service Taylor was later granted seven days remission.[15]

Constables Joseph Armstrong and Richard Furlong and their Native Assistants Fred and Harry were detailed to give chase to the absconders and left Perth before dawn on the following day.[16] On arriving at the scene of the escape Fred and Harry had no difficulty in picking up the tracks and the party set off in pursuit. However, late that afternoon the tracks were lost and every effort of the natives failed to pick them up again. Dejected, they returned to the Canning police station, where Constable Dunmall revived their spirits by informing them that both absconders had been at Palmer's place (where Joe had been working at the time of his arrest) the previous morning. Early on Thursday morning, now exactly two days behind the absconders, the police party headed for Palmer's, where they were told that Joe, accompanied by Evans, had called in to pick up a kangaroo skin rug and a pannikin he had left there on his arrest. The pair had rations for two or three days and Joe had acquired a tomahawk, some nails and a chart, and had said that if he had a gun and a kangaroo dog, he would be all right. This was a claim Joe was to make often during later escapes and it was said more as a plain statement of fact than with any thought of boasting. Joe had supreme confidence in his ability to outwit police and trackers and survive for long periods in the bush. He would later prove this to the entire colony, but for the moment capture seemed imminent.

Joe had told Palmer that he and Evans were going to leave the colony but both were on foot, with mounted police hot on their trail. Things looked grim. Then by pure chance unseasonal rain washed their tracks out and the police party were again prevented from following them up. After searching vainly about for traces of the tracks, Armstrong and Furlong decided to separate: the former, with Native Assistant Fred, headed down the road towards Pinjarra, while Furlong and Harry took the Albany road.

Armstrong did not get far southwards. His horse went lame before they reached Wungong and they were forced to camp there for the night. After questioning some folk from the Serpentine River who passed by, Armstrong decided against going any further south and next morning headed for an old sandalwood track which ran between Kelmscott and Beverley. His hunch proved correct. Fred found the tracks of Joe and Evans about 30 kilometres east of Kelmscott, from where they were traced, with much difficulty, for a further 10 kilometres eastwards. The fugitives were making every effort to conceal their tracks and eventually Fred lost them again. On the 11th he and Armstrong continued along the old wheel ruts to the Dale River, where they heard from settlers that Furlong and Harry, in company with Constable William Regan and his native tracker, had passed through a short time before. They caught up with Furlong and party at Fisher's place at Boyadine.

Furlong had gone down the Albany road only as far as the '36 Mile Station', where Regan was in charge. Regan was convinced that the absconders had headed eastwards,[17] and next morning had accompanied Furlong through the bush to strike the old sandalwood track and follow it towards Beverley.

On the 12th Armstrong headed for Beverley to have his horse shod, while Furlong and Regan began a systematic round of settlers' homesteads, hoping for some news of the runaways. They were joined by Constable Charles Barron and a keen young officer named

Hayden, but to no avail. Eventually Furlong finished his tour with a sweep along the Hotham River, Wandering Brook and the Bannister River, returning to Perth on the 18th, having heard nothing of the absconders, while Armstrong made enquiries around Beverley with a similar result and then returned to the Canning. Joe and his mate seemed to have disappeared into thin air.

In fact the next sighting of the absconders did not occur until almost two weeks after their escape. The relevant entry in the Newcastle Police Daily Occurrence Book reads [*verb. et lit.*]:

> 20th November 1865 — John Smith came to the station at 11 a.m. and reported that 2 men came to his shepherd at Bouben and make him leave his sheep out the camp untill a late hour this morning and told the shepherd to make them a damper. He done so and when the damper was done they cut it in 2 halfs and took one half with them. They called themselves Moondine Jo and one other man.[18]

This is one of the earliest references to Joe's nickname, which it appears he had adopted voluntarily, and the unlikely gesture of leaving the shepherd half the damper is typical of Joe's sense of fair play. The grammar in the report is no worse than others of that era. Educational standards were minimal and policemen were invariably men of action rather than words.

The following week Joe and Evans were reported to have called at the house of a man named Barndon and to have been carrying guns. Constables Monger and Wisbey set out in pursuit and word was relayed to York, where Constable Hayden was immediately despatched to take up the chase.[19] The latter was accompanied by two of the most outstanding native policemen ever known in Western Australia, Tommy Windich and Jemmy Mungaroo.[20]

Both of these trackers accompanied C. C. Hunt on his extensive explorations in 1866, and it was Tommy Windich who questioned wild natives near Koolyanobbing with regard to a party of white men supposedly killed by natives some years before. Jemmy, assisting J. H. Monger in exploration north-east of York two years later, retold this tale and the story was regarded as being a possible explanation of the fate of Ludwig Leichardt and his party. A government expedition led by John Forrest and including both Jemmy Mungaroo and Tommy Windich, set out the following year to search the area. It was this expedition that gave Forrest his big chance and also began his now famous association with Tommy Windich. Forrest found that the story probably originated from the eleven horses lost at Poison Rock by Robert Austin in 1854, and his opinion of the two native policemen is of interest. Jemmy he considered a first-class bushman, invaluable as a water finder, useful and obedient. His great failing was exaggeration and a tale never lost anything in his telling. Of Tommy Windich he could not speak too highly and it was Tommy that he chose to accompany him on his epic journey from Perth to Adelaide in 1870. Also on that trip was his brother Alexander Forrest who led an expedition of his own in 1871 and who also availed himself of the services of both Jemmy Mungaroo and Tommy Windich.[21] The latter accompanied the brothers on their best-known expedition when in 1874, after the failure of both Giles and Gosse to cross Western Australia's harsh central regions, the Forrest's party succeeded after fighting off wild natives at Weld Springs and experiencing much privation from want of water. But all this lay in the future for the two trackers as they led Constable Hayden on the trail of Joe and Evans.

On the first day of their search they called at the house of Thomas Reynolds at Flea Pool on the 'Salt River' (now known as the Mortlock River South), where they received information that the escapees had been there only the day before. Reynolds stated that the convicts had a black kangaroo dog and that the taller of the two had a loaded double-barrelled gun. Contemporary records prove that it was Joe who held the gun,[22] and his statement to Palmer on the Canning that given a gun and a 'roo dog he would be all right, will be recalled. Reynolds pointed out the direction taken by the fugitives and Hayden and his trackers pushed on.

The tracking was difficult and several times the trail was lost but Jemmy and Tommy persevered. The police horses suffered terribly from lack of water, yet Hayden pushing the whole party to the limit, on the third day succeeded in capturing the prisoners as they lay asleep at a place called Doodenanning, about 37 kilometres east of York. The double-barrelled gun was lying beside Evans, and Joe was reported as saying that if it had been beside him he would have shot Hayden with it;[23] nevertheless we can safely put this outburst down to his annoyance at being caught napping rather than any real desire to commit murder.

8 Saint Ronans Well

The return trip was exhausting for both police and prisoners. About 13 kilometres outside York Joe and Evans dropped to the ground and refused to walk any further. As their distress was genuine, a spring cart was hired by the police and sent out to fetch them.

The following day, a Sunday, was spent resting in the York lock-up and on the Monday they appeared before the resident magistrate of York, then Mr W. Cowan. The normal course of action for Cowan would have been to remand the prisoners to the Perth magistrates, but for some unknown reason Cowan dealt with the case himself. For absconding and being in possession of a firearm he sentenced them to twelve months in irons. This was considered a remarkably lenient sentence for bushrangers and drew surprised comment from the press and Captain Newland, the comptroller-general.[24] It is possible that Cowan was swayed by Joe's eloquence in protesting his innocence of the original charge, but whatever the reason, it is true that Joe and Evans got off extremely lightly. At the time no report had been received of their having committed any robberies in the York district, and only after they had been sentenced, it was learned that they had stolen the gun, a full shot belt, powder and gun caps from Joseph Carter. They were never charged with that theft.

One week later four policemen were detailed to escort Joe, Evans and eight other prisoners to Fremantle. What should have been a straightforward trip was protracted by Joe's falling sick. The police tried to put him up on one of their horses but he was too ill to ride and finally they had to stop a York-bound dray and ask the driver to turn his team and convey Joe as far as Saint Ronans Well. For this service the teamster, a man named Grindle, resumed his journey to York 5*s* richer, while the police were forced to spend the night camped at the well. Next morning Joe had made a remarkable recovery and the remainder of the journey was accomplished without incident.[25]

Substantial rewards of £5 to Police Constable Hayden and 30*s* each to the trackers were proposed by Captain Newland and authorized by the governor,[26] but then it was remembered that Joe was a colonial convict, and because the rewards now had to come from colonial, not imperial funds, they were cut to £1 for Hayden and 15*s* each for the trackers.[27] The comptroller-general was ordered to make certain in future that rewards were only recommended for the recovery of imperial convicts. The colonial coffers were indeed low.

REFERENCES

1. *Inquirer* 12 July 1865; *Perth Gazette* 7 July 1865.
2. Ibid.
3. Ibid.
4. *Perth Gazette* 7 July 1865.
5. Ibid.
6. Convict Records, WAA Acc. No. 1156 V14.
7. Ibid V23A.
8. *Perth Gazette* 29 September 1865.
9. Governor's Correspondence, 21 July 1865, WAA Acc. No. 136.
10. *Perth Gazette* 10 November 1865.
11. Police Records, WAA Acc. No. 129 8/464 & 8/450; *Perth Gazette* 10 November 1865, 5 January 1866.
12. Convict Records, WAA Acc. No. 1156 R&D5.
13. Ibid Acc. No. 128: *Racehorse* muster list.
14. Ibid Acc. No. 1156 R&D5.
15. Ibid Acc. No. 1156 C48 - 6072.
16. Police Records, WAA Acc. No. 129 8/499, 8/536.
17. Ibid 8/426.

18. Ibid Acc. No. 422, vol. 1.
19. Ibid Acc. No. 371 4.
20. Convict Records, WAA Acc. No. 1156 C48 - 6072.
21. Exploration Diaries, vol. 6, pp. 131-68, 214-20, 222-60, 264-325.
22. Convict Records, WAA Acc. No. 128: *Racehorse* muster list.
23. *Perth Gazette* 8 December 1865.
24. *Inquirer* 13 December 1865; Convict Records, WAA Acc. No. 1156 C48 - 6072.
25. Police Records, WAA Acc. No. 371 4.
26. Convict Records, WAA Acc. No. 1156 C48 - 6072.
27. Martin C. Carroll Jnr., Behind the Lighthouse, WAA PR6302.

Chapter six

1865-1866

Back in the Convict Establishment, this time weighed down with irons, Joe would have been interested to learn that Governor Hampton was now taking a personal interest in his case. Between Christmas Day and New Year's Day His Excellency had examined a deposition from Cowan, various police reports and Joe's penal history. He ordered a report to be made on both Joe and Evans on the expiry of their sentence of twelve months in irons.[1]

Hampton had been governor of the colony since February 1862, having previously held the position of comptroller-general in Tasmania. A report by a select committee inquiry into convict administration there in 1855 alleged that Hampton had engaged in corrupt practices, including the employment of convict labour for personal profit, and his interference in convict management in Western Australia had already provoked the hostility of local settlers. After the expiry of Colonel Henderson's term as comptroller-general, Hampton had assumed direct control of the Convict Department until the arrival of Captain Newland in 1863. Clashes between Newland and

9 Governor J. S. Hampton

10 Acting Comptroller-
General George Hampton

Hampton were frequent and it was claimed that the prevalence of prison breaks could be directly attributed to the governor's harshness. Hampton was not a popular governor, therefore when he succeeded in obtaining Newland's resignation in May 1866 and appointed his own son George as acting comptroller-general, the indignation of the local press was aroused. George Hampton already held several other salaried posts and it was felt that the governor was going too far.[2]

During this period, escape attempts continued unabated. Early in the New Year 1866 one convict managed to disappear from a chain gang during their early morning march between the Convict Establishment and the Fremantle Bridge works, and despite an extensive search no trace of him could be found. It is ironic to record that having escaped from the Convict Establishment, he should be captured inside the Perth Prison one night about a fortnight later. Having scaled the wall not far from a sentry box, he climbed onto the kitchen roof and lowered himself down the chimney with a rope. Once inside the kitchen he proceeded to obtain a supply of provisions, but was foolish enough to light a lamp which was seen by one of the guards and resulted in his capture. As the press put it, his 'ingenuity in making his escape, and adventurous entry into another prison, was rewarded by Mr. Leake with an addition of 12 months to his former sentence to the chain gang.'[3]

On 10 April a petition from Joe was forwarded to Captain New-

11 Main cell block, Fremantle Prison

land. Exactly what the missive contained is now unknown but it must have been strong stuff, as the chief justice promptly recommended a remission of four years. This was approved by Governor Hampton and Joe was informed of the result on 16 April.[4] The granting of this remission indicates that serious doubts regarding Joe's guilt were beginning to arise in the minds of officialdom. To Joe's way of thinking the result left much to be desired since it meant that, after completing his sentence of twelve months in irons, he still had nearly six years of his original sentence to serve.

About a fortnight after Joe received this unsatisfactory reply, a mass escape was plotted by the Fremantle Bridge chain-gang. The prisoners intended to take advantage of the absence of the pensioner guards who were in Fremantle collecting their pay. They planned to steal arms and ammunition from the pensioners' houses abutting the bridge approaches and then seize one of the ships lying at anchor in Gage Roads.[5] The plot was foiled by its premature discovery by prison authorities, but that the Fremantle Bridge work party were a determined bunch was evidenced by a newspaper report some ten weeks later. 'The convicts employed at the Fremantle Bridge are again amusing themselves and the police by seizing every chance of bolting, several instances having lately occurred, soon however terminating in recapture.'[6]

Soon after this Joe decided on another escape, and 23 July 1866 saw Superintendent Lefroy penning the following lines to the new acting comptroller-general, George Hampton.

> Sir,
>
> I have the honour to report that, at about 10 p.m. on the night of
> Saturday the 21st Inst., the Officers on night duty in the Cellular
> Division discovered that Col. Convict 8189 J. B. Johns had partially
> perforated two holes in the door of his cell with a view to the removal
> of the lock. Johns having been at once removed to the Refractory
> Cells, the following tools were found in his possession, namely 1 file,
> 1 small knife with the back thereof indented so as to serve the
> purpose of a saw, 1 pick lock and 1 of the hinge hooks wrenched
> from his cell table.[7]

A few days later Joe was brought before the visiting magistrate
and sentenced to a further six months in irons.[8] However this only
served to make him more determined than ever to escape.

One of the few successful escapes from the colony up to that time
had been made in late 1862 by John Williams (see Chapter Four).
Williams was reconvicted under another name in England and again
sentenced to transportation to Western Australia. He now arrived
on the convict ship *Belgravia*, was immediately recognized by prison
authorities and 'restored to his old quarters with an addition of 12
months in irons and 100 lashes'.[9] Although escape by sea was favoured
by many prospective runaways, a few experienced bushmen among
the convicts, including Joe, believed the eastern colonies could be
reached by an overland route during a good season. The journey
had not been attempted since the epic trip made by Edward John
Eyre in 1841, but C. C. Hunt's explorations east of Lake Lefroy and
the construction of a line of wells to the new country were making
this escape route seem more feasible every day.

Joe was determined to escape again before the wet season ended
and his next attempt was made only seventeen days after entering
the refractory cells. Winter escapes were always preferable because
of the ease with which water could be obtained in the bush and the
possibility of rain obliterating tracks. On Wednesday 8 August 1866
Joe's sobriquet appeared in print for the first time. Under the head-
line 'Escapade from the Convict Establishment' were the following
lines:

> Between 1 and 2 o-clock yesterday morning the notorious Johns, alias
> "Moondyne Joe", escaped from his cell in the Convict Establishment.
> Up to the present hour no further tidings, we believe, have been

heard of him, and from his previous career in the bush we fear the police may have some trouble in his re-capture.[10]

The fears of the press were to be fully realized. Sergeant J. Regan was put in charge of the first search party to hunt for this 'desperate fellow',[11] as the *Perth Gazette* called Joe, and Regan's report, dated 13 August, tells the story [*verb. et lit.*]:

> I beg leave to report for the information of the Superintendent that myself, P.C. Fee and 2 natives were sent by Mr. Sub Inspector Snook on the morning of the 7th instant in search of Regt. No. 8189, Joseph B. Johns, alias Mondine Joe; we proceeded to the prison and seen where he got over the prison wall. Whilst searching for tracks there we recieved information that the tool shed at the bridge was broken into by some person. We proceeded to there, found the tracks which we followed towards Mr. Pince's Slaughter House. Found where he cut his irons with a chisel and sledge hammer which he had taken from the tool shed at the ferry. We then tracked him to the watch house on the hill where the flag staff is erected and found his tracks inside the house. The warder on duty there reported to us that a knife was taken away from there and the flag line cut and a part of it carried away. We then with great difficulty followed the tracks from there towards the convict establishment along by the asylum and through a quarry where a party of prisoners were at work and along an old road leading to the Canning getting on the track so as we could trot along at a quick pace.[12]

Here, Regan sent back one of the trackers who was on foot, and the mounted police party then followed the tracks at a canter, first to Bull Creek and then down-stream to the Canning Bridge, where Joe had crossed the river. Joe had been moving fast and had made no attempt to conceal his tracks until arriving at the bridge, where a multitude of other tracks could be counted upon to confuse the best of trackers. He then began to use more care. The police investigated a report that some person has broken into James Burns's house through a window, but could find no tracks leading away from the dwelling.

Regan's report continues [*verb. et lit.*]:

> Returned to the Bridge where we seen a track reacrossing the Bridge.

Believing it to be the same followed it when it led into Mr. . . . .'s
Paddock and found from all appearances that the party who made
the tracks laid in ambush. It then being dark camped a short distance
from the Bridge. On the morning of the 8th inst. found fresh tracks
at bridge which one of them appeared to be Johns' track and followed
them through Mr. Wellard's Paddock and along the riverside and
found that the parties had taken a boat and crossed the river, also
received information that two prisoners were seen about the place
that morning. The place mentioned that the prisoners were seen
there were no tracks and believed it to be a false information. We
then returned to the Canning where we again re-covered the tracks
and where Johns had been seen and had a conversation with a man
named McCloud and stated to him that he wanted a kangaroo dog
and gun and then that he would not care for any man. It then being
too dark to track we proceeded to the Canning Police Station making
enquiries among the settlers on our way and got no further account.
That night raining so heavy put all tracks out. On the morning of
the 9th instant P.C. Dunmall and his native started to visit all the
settlers along the Canning River. Myself, P.C. Fee and native visited
all Mr. Mason's sawyers at the Timber Station and could get no
account. On the 10th inst. visited Mr. Robbin's sheep station and
Baker's back of the close to the Helena River and Guildford and the
Eastward of the hills towards the Canning River, examining all the
cross roads for tracks. Met P.C. Dunmall and native in the hills after
visiting Mr. Batemans timber station and could find no tracks or
information about. We returned to the Canning Police Station that
night. On the 11th instant visited Mr. Hardy's sheep station on the
Canning Plains and returned to Fremantle.[13]

On the same day that Sergeant Regan was writing up his report
old William Dodd of Glenavon Farm visited the Newcastle police
station with a disturbing story. At 7.00 pm on the previous evening
he had opened his door in response to an insistent rapping, and Joe
with three other men, all in prison garb, had pushed their way past
him. Two of the men had kept guard over him while the others ransacked his house. They took his double-barrelled gun, a six-barrelled
revolver loaded in four barrels, some ammunition and flour, and
demanded clothing and money.[14] In Sergeant Kelly's words [*litteratim*], 'to compell his compliance one of them said he would nock
his brains out with a great bludgeon which he held over his head.'[15]

Again Joe's nickname appeared in print. An *Inquirer* correspondent at Northam wrote:

> Moondyne Joe and 3 other runaways broke fiercly into Dodd's the other night. They threw him on the bed, ordering him to be still under threats of further violence. The poor old man was very frightened and told them to take anything they wanted, but not to hurt his poor old woman, and for her he continued to beg earnestly. She, more courageous than him, pulled off her slipper and began pitching into the fellows that held Dodd down.[16]

Another report stated that 'Mrs. Dodd strongly objected to their taking away her husbands arms and one of the men proposed "settling" her, but Joe forbid [*sic*] his touching the old lady.'[17]

Joe's companions were John James, Thomas Bugg and John Bassett, absconders from the Greenmount road party. All three had arrived on the convict ship *Racehorse* in August the previous year, and it will be recalled that John James was the partner of David Evans, Joe's companion on his previous escape. Just how James, Bugg and Bassett made their escape and teamed up with Joe is not recorded but it was definitely no accident.

All three were shorter than Joe and of medium build. James was thirty-five, about Joe's age, while Bugg was two years younger and Bassett only twenty-three.[18] Joe's knowledge of bushcraft made him the obvious leader of the little gang which was destined to become a real thorn in Governor Hampton's side. Newspapers dubbed them 'Moondyne Joe and Co.', and continual reports of their exploits were to make Joe's name a household word throughout the colony.

Since at Dodd's their demands for clothing were fruitless, they voiced their intentions of stealing some from the stores in town. Apprised of this, Government Resident Durlacher posted guards at the approaches to Newcastle with instructions to alert the police quietly if the bushrangers were seen, but without result. The following day Police Constables Wheeler and Kirk with two native assistants departed from Newcastle to pick up the trail of the absconders at Mokine, south-west of Northam, Sergeant Kelly having heard from an old Aboriginal woman that the gang were headed in that direction. Constable Wisbey of the Mokine police station was informed of what was going on and ordered to be on the lookout.

Durlacher had great hopes that the measures adopted would be instrumental in capturing the runaways, and Sergeant Kelly was also confident, if somewhat disappointed at not being able to take part in the chase personally. He wrote [*verb. et lit.*]:

> I am satisfied that if the police once get on their tracks they will soon run them up and all seem determined and are well armed while the old gun and old revolver they took from Dodd are comparatively speaking worthless. I should very mutch like to be with the police that are after them but I could neither hire nor borrow a horse — besides we have 7 prisoners in the lockup and I am obliged to keep P.C. Monaghan in charge of them. 2 of them are natives in for murder and they are all the time picking at their locks, chains or the sell walls trying to get away.[19]

When Constable McAtee arrived from Guildford the next day to assist in the search, Kelly wanted to take his horse and go to Northam to make enquiries, but McAtee was reluctant to loan the animal and set out for Northam himself, leaving Kelly fuming at being deskbound. Kelly's chance for action came the day after, when he accompanied Durlacher on a round of the settlers residing between Newcastle and Northam.[20] Nothing had been heard of Joe. On their way home they met the police party, under McAtee, who were also visiting settlers. McAtee had found Wheeler, Kirk and Wisbey at Northam, whither they had regressed after unsuccessful search at Mokine, and that morning, leaving Wisbey at Northam, he, Wheeler and Kirk, accompanied by Constable Moan of York and their native assistants, had gone to Dodd's place. The natives had spent three hours trying to pick up the tracks, but because three days had elapsed since the robbery, they were unsuccessful.[21] Kelly gave them instructions to search Cave Hill, the 'Salt Valley' (probably the Mortlock River North) and then Moondyne. He and Durlacher then returned to Newcastle.

That night Kelly had a visit from an informer. His report reads in part:

> I have been confidentially informed by Thomas Penifather, a sawyer on the Toodyay Road who is the most intimate and confidential friend in this district to the absconder Joseph Johns. Penifather says that about 1 a.m. on 11 inst. Johns and 3 other men came to his

house and told him that they were going to take Dodd's arms and
with them they would be able to take away all the police arms and
ammunition. They would take the R.M.'s money and arms and
that they would then break into one of the stores in this town
and get a fitout of clothing and money; that they would then
rest for a day or so at Moondine and go overland to the new
North Country. He further said he would call again and see Penifather in which case Penifather said he would come in directly and
let me know.[22]

Kelly noted Joe's grandiose plans and congratulated himself for
instructing the police party to search around Moondyne.

Meanwhile the police slept that night at Ferguson's place, splitting
into two parties the following morning and reuniting in the evening
at Carter's place at Jennacubbine, where Joe had stolen the gun and
ammunition on his previous jaunt in the bush. Here they instigated
night-watches, looking out for the glow of a campfire amongst the
surrounding hills. Next day they separated as before, heading by
different routes towards Northam.

That same day, the 18th, Kelly apparently spoke with his increas-
ingly-nervous informant. He wrote to the superintendent: 'Peni-
fathers statement had better be kept perfectly secret as he says that
his life will be the forfeit if it is made known.'[23]

On the 19th the police party went in to Northam, where they
separated, Moan returning to York, Wheeler and Kirk heading for
the Mortlock River and McAtee going back to Newcastle, where he
learned of Penifather's statement for the first time. Next day he
went after Wheeler and Kirk with orders to search the Moondyne
hills. This was the last Kelly was to hear of his constables for over a
week.

That afternoon Kelly received a report that Frazer's place had
been broken into and some kangaroo skins and a shirt stolen. He
immediately raced to the scene to search for tracks only to find the
ground so hard that no traces could be found. Two days later Mrs
Caroline Roser reported that the absconders had visited her place
that morning demanding food and ammunition. This was too much
for Kelly, who borrowed two horses from Durlacher and with Constables Wisbey, Bishop and Monaghan galloped out in search of the
bushrangers.[24]

REFERENCES

1. Convict Records, WAA Acc. No. 1156 C48 - 6072.
2. *Perth Gazette* 11 May 1866.
3. Ibid 19 January 1866.
4. Convict Records, WAA Acc. No. 1156 C49 - 6087.
5. *Perth Gazette* 4 May 1866.
6. Ibid 13 July 1866.
7. Convict Records, WAA Acc. No. 1156 C32 - 114.
8. Ibid C50 - 7464.
9. *Perth Gazette* 27 July 1866, 16, 23 August 1867.
10. *Inquirer* 8 August 1866.
11. *Perth Gazette* 10 August 1866.
12. Police Records, WAA Acc. No. 129 9/615.
13. Ibid.
14. Resident Magistrate of Newcastle to Colonial Secretary, 15 August 1866, WAA CS0583.
15. Police Records, WAA Acc. No. 422, vol. 2.
16. *Inquirer* 22 August 1866.
17. *Perth Gazette* 17 August 1866.
18. Convict Records, WAA Acc. No. 128: *Racehorse* muster list.
19. Police Records, WAA Acc. No. 129 9/649.
20. Ibid Acc. No. 422, vol. 2.
21. Ibid Acc. No. 129 9/802.
22. Ibid 9/719.
23. Ibid.
24. Ibid Acc. No. 422, vol. 2.

Chapter seven

August-
September 1866

After Joe's escape from the Convict Establishment a full military investigation had been undertaken in an attempt to prevent further breakouts. The military authorities considered the lighting of the prison yard to be insufficient, and as a result experiments were conducted with newfangled kerosine lamps. These were eventually adopted throughout the prison and were retained until the advent of electric light.[1] While these experiments were occupying prison staff, Joe continued to lead the police a merry dance around Newcastle.

Kelly and his hastily-assembled band, put onto a false trail at Roser's, wasted the whole of their first day of the chase diligently tracking two sawyers.[2] They finally found the correct tracks the following day, leading over hills so rough and stony that the police were forced to dismount and track on their hands and knees.[3] Joe and his companions were found to be on foot, leading a horse. Only 11 kilometres were covered before nightfall and Kelly was thoroughly disgusted with the tracking abilities of Wisbey's native assistant, the only tracker with the party. He decided to send Monaghan back to

Newcastle to ask the resident magistrate to release one of the native murderers from prison to assist in the search.

The party got onto easier ground next day, but Kelly's expectations were dashed when a police constable named Campbell galloped up with orders from Subinspector William Roper Piesse to remain where he was and await Piesse's arrival. Kelly fumed, but there was nothing for it except to do as he was ordered. Piesse rode up soon afterwards with Constable Fee and four native assistants. After hearing Kelly's report he ordered both the sergeant and Constable Bishop back to Newcastle police station and took over command of the party which now numbered three constables and five trackers. An exasperated Kelly was again deskbound.

Subinspector Piesse came from Guildford, where news had been received a few days previously that Mr G. Sewel's stable on 'Chittering Brook' had been entered and a saddle, three bridles and a stock-whip had been stolen. Both Sewel and Piesse were convinced that this was the work of Joe and his companions, but the Guildford police were all out on patrol and the station was manned only by Sergeant Peacock.[4] Piesse had explained the situation to the superintendent of police, with the result that Constable Fee from Fremantle and his Native Assistant Bob were instructed to proceed to Newcastle to man that station in Kelly's absence. Piesse and Constable Campbell followed the next day.

On arrival at Newcastle Piesse asked Mr Drummond for a loan of his two natives Alick and Sam, but was informed that they were at York. He finally procured the services of Police Trackers Tobey and Charcoal and was preparing to mount his own party in pursuit of the bushrangers when Monaghan arrived with Kelly's request to release one of the native murderers. Piesse was opposed to this move and ordered Monaghan to take over duties at the station the following morning when he, Fee and Campbell went to join Kelly's party.[5] Piesse was certainly the senior man and had a perfect right to take over Sergeant Kelly's party as he did, but one can understand Kelly's chagrin at, as he put it, losing the sport of catching them after all his trouble.[6]

Although Kelly considered that the party had reached 'first rate tracking ground', Piesse reported it as some of the worst country he had seen.[7] Whichever the case, heavy rain the following day washed out all traces of the tracks, and although Piesse and his party scoured the country around Northam and Mokine, then across to Spring Hill and the Mortlock River, the tracks were not met with again.

Finally the police proceeded to Clackline and the day after visited a sawyer's camp between the Northam and Newcastle roads, then headed across to Deepdale in the Avon valley. That evening, the 29th, the party, tired, hungry and dispirited, returned to Newcastle police station, where Kelly took much pleasure in informing Piesse that McAtee's party had captured one of the bushrangers two days previously and were hard on the heels of the others. McAtee had found Joe's base camp and succeeded in capturing young Bassett.

On meeting Constables Kirk and Wheeler at James Sinclair's place near 'the Ti-tree Swamp' on the 20th, McAtee had informed them of Penifather's statement and the party had headed towards the Moondyne hills in the hope of picking up the bushrangers' tracks. On the way, at McKnoe's place, they were joined by Constable Lally of the Bailup station and split into two parties. They then proceeded to Gee's place, where they planned to halt for the night. By pure luck Wheeler's party came across the bushrangers' tracks not far from Gee's at 8.00 pm, and the following morning the chase began. The events leading up to Bassett's capture are best related in McAtee's own words [*verb. et lit.*]:

22nd August 1866 — At 8.00 am Started on the tracks which we followed to the Bald Hill, one in the Moondyne Range. Owing to it's uncommon rocky nature and night closing in we losed the tracks. Halted for the night at Morgan's sheep station in the hills at 7.00 pm having visited 5 of Joe's old traps and haunts.

23rd August 1866 — At 8.00 am left camp and proceeded towards the upper Chittering, scowering the hills and visiting 3 of James Everett's stations. Halted for the night at Julimar Spring, a former trap of Joe's. Kept watch during this and the preceding night looking out for fires etc.

24th August 1866 — At 8.00 a.m. left camp. Proceeded towards the lower Chittering via R. Spice's, H. Morley's, H. Martin's, James Anderson's . . . farm scowering the hills and making diligent enquiry as we went. Heard nothing of the bushrangers. Halted for the night at Anderson's flat at 7.00 p.m.

25th August 1866 — At 7.00 a.m. left camp. Proceeded towards the

Upper Swan scowering as we went. At G. Sewel's we were informed
that on the evening of the 19th at 7.00 p.m., a saddle and 3 bridles
had been stolen out of his stable. We halted and after 3 hours
diligent search succeeded in finding Joe's tracks close to the stable
which the natives were unable to follow. We halted for the night
near the junction of the brook with the Avon River which, flowing
together, forms the River Swan.* At 9.00 p.m., Wheeler, 1 native
and I proceeded on foot to the top of one of the hills in the Moondyne
Range in hopes of seeing a fire. Returned to camp at 12.00 midnight.

26th August 1866 — At 8.00 a.m. left camp and proceeded to scower
the western range, forming 2 parties. We fell across the tracks of
men and one horse freshly made at the Junction. We followed them
till 1.00 p.m. when, heavy rain setting in, we could follow them no
further. Wheeler and party joined us at 5.00 p.m. We found, in an
old hut, a gun cap box containing 24 gun wads. Night setting in, we
halted in this old hut at 6.00 p.m., having, after the rain abated,
scowered in the neighbourhood of the Junction.[8]

The police were weary, damp and dispirited. The never-ceasing
sound of the rushing river was getting on their nerves. They were
completely closed in by immense, bush-covered hills, and frequent
heavy showers seemed to give them little hope of ever getting close
to Joe. In fact Joe was just around the corner on the other side of
Jumperkine Hill and the following day would see the police twice
come close to catching him. The tale is resumed by Constable
McAtee.

27th August 1866 — At 6.30 a.m. left camp and, picking up the track,
followed it, to do which was very difficult and tedious. At 10.00
a.m., we heard the report of a gun and hastened towards whence
came the sounds. At 11.00 a.m. came upon the camp of the bushrangers situated in a very deep ravine in which ran two small brooks
forming the letter "V", in the point of which was advantageously
pitched the nest of the absconders. Forming a half circle we, Wheeler,
Kirk, Lally and I, with 2 natives, closed round the nest as fast as the
roughness of the ground would permit.

* Author's note. In 1967 the Nomenclature Advisory Committee agreed that the
Swan River commenced where Wooroloo Brook meets the main stream, thus revert-
ing to the original surveys carried out by Philip Chauncy in 1843, but for many years
the rivers appeared on maps as mentioned by Constable McAtee.

The roughness of this ravine can be seen from Walyunga Lookout. The brook tumbles into the Avon just west of Jumperkine Hill and it is easy to imagine the difficulties of the police, sliding and stumbling on the steep, wet slopes, trying to co-ordinate their movements so that all should arrive at the camp simultaneously. They managed it without being seen or heard, and McAtee continues:

> The nest contained, to our great disappointment, one man, Bassett, only. Him we arrested and took charge of all the camp contained consisting of 1 horse, 1 saddle, 2 bridles, 1 double-barrelled gun, 5 or 6 lbs. of lead, 12 gun balls, 2 or 3 lbs. tobacco and many other things too numerous to mention. In this ravine we halted for an hour during which time we were in hops to get such information from the captured as would lead to the arrest of the others of the gang. I, with the natives scowered on foot the neighbourhood of the camp and found tracks of 3 men leading towards the Swan. . . . having got from Bassett information to the effect that Joe and the others had gone to do robberies, one in Fremantle and another near Freshwater Bay, and that they would not return til Saturday night, 1st of September, at 12 noon we started on the tracks, Bassett having declared that they had started an hour only before his arrest and that they would go by Cruse's Mill and remain that night and next day in that locality. We followed their tracks for quite 18 miles and, shortly after sundown, came upon their camp which was only partly made and in which we found 1 large pocketbook, 2 pair slippers made of possum skins, 1 large knife very sharp in point and edge and a saw on the back, a piece of damper which, having had nothing to eat from the morning of the 26th save a few ounces of damper, we soon made use of. The bushrangers had, on hearing us cross the brook at the base of the hill on which they were halted, decamped. After an hours fruitless search, proceeded to Mr. Fawell's some 2 or 2½ miles from where we were. We were obliged to do so for the purpose of getting some food. Halted at 8.00 p.m.

It had been a close call for Joe, and reporting the capture of Bassett the *Perth Gazette* was confident that the rounding up of the whole gang was imminent.[9] This paper also mentioned a rumour that another runaway had joined Joe's gang but no evidence in support of this was found by the police. The pocketbook found by McAtee's party was claimed to contain a journal of Joe's proceedings and a list of articles required for a lengthy expedition. This would now be a relic of great value but inquiries by the author have so far failed to bring to light any clue regarding its fate.

The possum-skin slippers, found in the bushrangers' hurriedly-abandoned camp were a common part of Joe's bush apparel. They served as an alternative to convict boots which were distinctly marked with a broad arrow design on the soles. The slight tracks left by the slippers were difficult to follow, and possums being easy to find and trap, the time spent fashioning several pairs of moccasins from the skins was well worth it for any convict on the run. As alternative footwear Joe also used strips of raw cowhide tied over his boots with leather thongs. These served not only to disguise the broad arrow design, but also to prevent excessive wear. Another favourite of his were moccasins of sheep skin with the wool on the outside.

Next day McAtee detailed Wheeler to escort Bassett and the stolen property to Guildford. The horse found with Bassett was the property of Alexander Warren, proprietor of the Bush Inn. Warren's bell was still around its neck though the clapper had been removed by the bushrangers. McAtee and the rest of the party followed up the tracks. They found that Joe, James and Bugg had walked out to the Guildford road, where they had donned their soft slippers and walked along the road, crossed the Upper Swan Bridge and then turned back towards the Avon valley. The police slept that night at Warren's, and early the following morning resumed the chase as far as 'The Junction'.

But Joe and his mates, by forcing themselves to keep on the march, and helped by the rugged nature of the Moondyne country, were gradually outdistancing the police. They rested that night in what McAtee, when he found the place next day, described as a 'frightful ravine'. By now the police were again short of rations and Lally and Kirk, with one native tracker, were detailed to head for Bailup for supplies, whilst McAtee and Wheeler, with two trackers, kept up the pursuit.

Lally and Kirk, loaded with supplies, left Bailup to rejoin the chase late in the afternoon of the following day, but before they had proceeded far, a messenger caught up with them with orders to return. Reluctantly abandoning the quest to ease their companions' growling bellies, they turned back to find that Subinspector Piesse had arrived at the station and desired news of the progress of the hunt.

Having learned of Bassett's capture two days previously, Piesse, accompanied by Constables Fee and Campbell and three native trackers, had proceeded down the Avon from Newcastle in hopes of falling in with McAtee's party.[10] Although admitting that neither himself, his constables nor his trackers, had any knowledge of the bush in that area, Piesse was determined to place himself in charge of McAtee's party.[11] Nothing could have suited Joe better. The subinspector detained Lally and Kirk at Bailup police station until the following morning, when the whole party set out to overtake McAtee's hungry little band. When they finally caught up they were disappointed to find that heavy rain during the night had washed out all the tracks.

McAtee had stuck to the tracks doggedly while awaiting the arrival of rations. The bushrangers had changed their footwear several times, negotiated the highest and roughest hills in the ranges and crossed the turbulent Avon on poles. Although the tracks had been lost, the police had succeeded in finding two of the bushrangers' supply caches. Stowed away in hollow trees were two saddle-packs and a large bag of flour. Joe's forethought in providing himself with hidden supply dumps, probably scattered all through the bush in that area, explains how the bushrangers could move with such speed. The flour had been disturbed some three days previously and Piesse had suspicions that it might have been poisoned. He gave orders not to touch it. Whether or not it was poisoned is not known, but these suspicions effectively denied the police any advantages from their finds. The whole party, now consisting of seven police and six natives camped that night at a place in the hills known as 'Wardingbob-bing'.

The next three days were spent fruitlessly searching the rugged hills and deep ravines along the Avon valley. Finally Piesse decided to cross the country towards the York road and he, Campbell and Fee separated from McAtee's party. Lally and Wheeler, with Native Tracker Johnny Buckskin, headed into Newcastle to have their horses shod, the rugged going having taken its toll. They took with them Dodd's double-barrelled gun and shot belt, both of which had been found on Bassett.[12] Only McAtee and Kirk, with the assistance of two trackers, remained to continue the search along the Avon valley.

Piesse and his party arrived at Lloyd's '19 Mile Inn' on the York

road in the late afternoon of 6 September and were immediately
regaled with stories of the bushrangers' recent exploits near York.
Joe and his gang were supposed to have returned to Dodd's place
and committed robberies at Knott's place and Mr Hamersley's shepherd's hut. Piesse decided to stay the night at the inn and make an
early start for those places the following morning in hopes of getting
onto fresh tracks. Later that evening however, a party of York
police, escorting three prisoners, arrived at the inn and were able to
assure Piesse that the tales were untrue. The subinspector considered
it useless to be wearing the horses out to no avail and made up his
mind to give up the search, let his men take over the prisoners and
return to Guildford the following morning. This would enable the
York police to return to their station in case the bushrangers did
make an appearance there.

Piesse left rather late next morning, calling at the Prince of
Wales Inn at Mahogany Creek about noon, where he was informed
that a convict had absconded the previous night from a timber-
cutting party based nearby. He visited the camp and questioned the
officer in charge. The absconder turned out to be Henry Kingston
who, it may be recalled, was suspected of assisting Joe in his escape
from the old Toodyay lockup five years earlier. In all probability,
Kingston had ideas of joining up with Joe and his gang, but Joe was
a long way from his old haunts by this time. Piesse kept a lookout
for tracks on his way towards Greenmount, but eventually proceeded
on to Guildford and left the pursuit of Kingston up to Constable
Allely, having found that officer following the supposed tracks of
the absconder in the dark near Greenmount. He later found out
that Kingston had been captured by a native assistant near Lloyd's
inn earlier that same day.[13]

During the subinspector's absence the residents of Guildford had
followed Joe's career in the newspapers and speculated with some
excitement on the possibility of the bushrangers visiting one of their
homesteads. There was no real fear of Joe and his gang who were
generally considered harmless. In fact, by the time Piesse returned
from his luckless pursuit, the Guildford correspondent of the *Inquirer*
had mentioned in his column that Moondyne Joe and his companions
had given place as topics of conversation to 'anticipation respecting
the result of the cricket match between the married and single

members of the club'.[14] Another article concerning the bushrangers in the same weekly newspaper ended: 'it is not at all likely that the vagabonds will long escape the clutches of the constables.' This opinion was widely held, and in fact only the day after Piesse and his men had separated from McAtee's party, Kirk and McAtee had found fresh tracks. Piesse appears to have been somewhat of a Jonah where Joe was concerned.

McAtee and Kirk stuck grimly to the trail, their trackers often down on their hands and knees, and were joined on Thursday, September 6, by Constable Wheeler and Tracker Johnny Buckskin on freshly-shod horses. Wheeler reported that Constable Lally had returned to Bailup police station and that great excitement was being caused in Newcastle by the presence of Governor Hampton on an official visit. The governor had arrived two days previously, had inspected the new lockup and police station and seemed well pleased.[15] No doubt the three constables speculated on their chances of capturing the bushrangers and bringing them triumphantly into Newcastle during the governor's stay, but Joe and his gang were being sadly underestimated.

Joe was determined to attempt an overland escape to South Australia before the winter rains ended. A large amount of clothing, supplies and ammunition would be required for such an arduous journey, and to this end he was planning the biggest and most audacious robbery of his career. Even at gunpoint the struggling outlying settlers would be unable to provide the mass of equipment he needed. No, the only course was to rob a store. James Everett had ruined Joe's horse-trapping business by buying up the land around his horse traps and Everett owned the largest store in the now almost-deserted old town of Toodyay (now West Toodyay). Joe was never in doubt about whose store he should rob.

REFERENCES

1. Convict Records, WAA Acc. No. 1156 C50-7573.
2. Police Records, WAA Acc. No. 422, vol. 2.
3. Ibid Acc. No. 129 9/744.
4. Ibid 9/668.
5. Ibid 9/750.

6. Ibid 9/744.
7. Ibid 9/750.
8. Ibid 9/802.
9. *Perth Gazette* 31 August 1866.
10. Police Records, WAA Acc. No. 422, vol. 2.
11. Ibid Acc. No. 129 9/750.
12. Ibid Acc. No. 422, vol. 2.
13. Ibid Acc. No. 371 5.
14. *Inquirer* 5 September 1866.
15. Police Records, WAA Acc. No. 422, vol. 2.

Chapter eight

September-
October 1866

The tracks followed by McAtee and his party brought them ever closer to old Toodyay until the evening of Friday 7 September 1866, when they met Sergeant Kelly and a group of natives following tracks leading away from the town. In angry tones Kelly informed McAtee that a daring robbery had taken place two nights previously. James Everett's store had been ransacked and guns, ammunition, clothing and supplies valued at over £50 had been stolen. To make matters worse the robbery had taken place during the governor's visit.[1] Poor Kelly. One can imagine his feelings. The audacity of the crime had made him look a fool and he was determined to bring the culprits to book.

News of the robbery had been brought to the police station by a man named John Edwards at 6.00 am on Thursday morning.[2] Within minutes Kelly, with Native Tracker Dickey, was following Edwards to the scene. He found the place a complete shambles: boxes had been broken open and their contents strewn all over the floor; papers, books and stores had been knocked down and interior doors prised open. The caretaker, Robert Mathews, was not sure just how much was missing, but had already noted the loss of three pairs of boots, two double-barrelled guns, some gun caps and shot, and quantities of tea, sugar and bacon. He had heard someone in the store shortly after midnight but had been too frightened to give the alarm. An examination of the store showed that one of the bars over a window had been unscrewed at the top and forced to one side, but no tracks could be found. Disconsolate, Kelly returned to the station.

Everett was away on one of his properties at the time, so Kelly sent someone to fetch him. On his arrival Everett was asked if he had any idea who had committed the robbery. A man of many enemies, Everett promptly named three suspects.[3] The sergeant procured warrants to search the houses of these people and next day all three warrants were executed. Nothing was found. Eventually late that afternoon Kelly found the tracks of three men leading away from the old town, and suspecting that these could be the thieves, set off in pursuit. He was not on the trail long before he met McAtee.

After hearing Kelly's tale of woe, McAtee and his men dismounted and examined the tracks he was following. These were recognized immediately as those of the bushrangers, even though Joe and his mates were now wearing new light slippers. As by this time it was getting dark, the police returned to the Newcastle police station for the night.

At 9.00 am next morning, refreshed and re-equipped, McAtee, Kirk and Wheeler, with three native assistants, returned to the tracks to resume the chase. Kelly sat down to prepare a report and inventory of the property stolen from Everett's. The end result was quite an imposing list, including flash new clothes for all three bush rangers and almost everything they could need for a lengthy expedition. (The complete list is given in Appendix A.) It is possible that this robbery influenced Everett to announce publicly only a fortnight later his intention of relinquishing his business as a general store-keeper.[4]

While Kelly was writing his report, Police Constable Hayden and his native assistant arrived at Newcastle. Hayden, who was on the trail of an absconder named Jones, suspected of joining the bushrangers, had an hour's rest at the police station and then set out to join McAtee's party.[5] A three hours' ride brought him up with them, but to his disappointment the tracks had been lost.

McAtee's party spent the next two days searching for traces of Joe and his mates to the east, north and north-west of Newcastle but they had no success.[6] Eventually they were forced to return to Newcastle to have three of the horses shod. Sergeant Kelly was convinced that the bushrangers, having got all they wanted at Everett's would not be likely to remain in the vicinity.[7] He gave orders for Hayden to return to his station at Youndegin 64 kilometres east of York, then the easternmost police outpost in the colony, and sent the Newcastle police, McAtee, Kirk and Wheeler, across to Northam, where they were to be joined by Constable Wisbey. They would then circle out behind Northam and Newcastle and across to the Victoria Plains, making a careful search and enquiry as they went. If the bushrangers had headed east, Kelly reasoned, McAtee and party must cut their tracks.

McAtee disagreed. He had a feeling that Joe and his mates were hiding not far from Newcastle, and his unhappiness with his orders is evident in his journal. After all, Joe was no idiot and the police were doing precisely what he would expect them to. But orders were orders and Kelly's instructions were followed to the letter. After four days' searching they found fresh tracks of three men, one mounted on a horse. They followed these for about 10 kilometres but were disappointed to learn that the men were in the employ of Mr Chidlow. That night they were informed that a policeman had passed through the area on the previous day and left word that the police party were to return to Newcastle at once.

McAtee's hunch had proved correct. During the absence of the Newcastle police 'the firm of Moondyne Joe and Company', as the press were now calling the gang, had struck again. On the morning of Wednesday 12 September the bushrangers, decked out in their new finery, had descended on the hut of Alfred Larwood, one of Everett's timber splitters working near Moondyne Spring. There Joe acquired what he had always considered a necessity for life in the bush, a good kangaroo dog. The gang also took supplies of flour, salted pork, tea and sugar before disappearing back into the bush.[8] That night, no doubt aware that the bulk of the Newcastle police were away on patrol, the gang called at William Roser's place again and took a double-barrelled gun. They also forced Roser's son to remove his boots, apparently for one of the gang who had not obtained a good fit at Everett's store. Before leaving, Joe added Roser's kangaroo dog to his party. Now they were fully equipped to pioneer an overland escape route to South Australia.

Joe had put a great deal more thought into this attempt than just equipping his party. He was well aware that Charles Hunt was exploring the unknown wilderness to the eastward and, to provide water for the gang, he relied on Hunt's programme of constructing permanent wells along his route. On catching up with Hunt and his party Joe intended to surprise them at night and take their horses and rations at gunpoint. He and his gang would then destroy what horses they did not need, thus forcing Hunt to walk back to civilization.[9] With the resulting head start Joe hoped to be over the border before the news broke. To prevent the police from becoming aware of his departure from the Newcastle district Joe had arranged to be 'seen' in the vicinity for some weeks to come. His plans were very nearly successful and only bad luck was to prevent his undertaking what would have been a supreme test of his bushmanship. Hunt himself was already experiencing difficulty from dry conditions on the Hampton Plains, and in fact it was to be another nine years before the desolate region between Hunt's furthest east (near Lake Roe) and South Australia would be conquered by Ernest Giles who suffered incredible hardships through want of water.

As Joe and his mates headed ever deeper into gimlet and salmon-gum country, James Everett called at the Newcastle police station and reported that some of the property stolen from his store had been found planted in the bush near Mr Tucker's. Kelly borrowed a horse, there being no police horses in the stables, and went out to investigate.[10] The few items found (see Appendix B) had apparently been dumped by Joe as being excess weight or were perhaps stashed there to be collected by friends. Joe may even have hoped that the police would expect him to return to the cache and would waste manpower in setting up an ambush. If any men at all had been available, it is possible that Kelly may have considered such a move, but, with all his men out on patrol, Kelly decided to convey the stolen goods back to the police station. Shortly after Kelly's return,

McAtee and his police party trooped in. During their absence Piesse had learnt of the shortage of police in Newcastle and had again been ordered into the fray by the superintendent.[11]

Next day, the 16th, Constables Wisbey, McAtee, Kirk and four trackers headed west to carry out a further search of the Avon valley, where that afternoon they were joined by Piesse from Guildford with Constables Hyde, Allely, Lally and one tracker. After wasting some time trailing three men and a dog who turned out to be teamsters searching for their bullocks, Piesse left Thomas Allely with the Newcastle police, divided them into two parties, and after instructing them to search the country carefully, proceeded on to Newcastle. The subinspector spent the following day organizing a dozen local Aborigines into pairs with instructions to roam the bush in search of the bushrangers. In the event of sighting the gang or coming across their tracks, one native was to remain on the trail while the other went for the police. To ensure the loyalty of his sable bloodhounds Piesse supplied them generously with provisions and promised them a reward should they find the fugitives. In reporting these activities to the superintendent, Piesse stated that he had reason to believe the absconders were not many miles from Newcastle. It seems that Joe's forethought in arranging for the police to be supplied with false information after his departure was paying off.

Piesse and his party left Newcastle on Tuesday the 18th and headed back down the Avon valley but they were unable to catch up with McAtee's party. The latter group had turned northwards up the Brockman River, and, following a party of strangers seen by settlers and suspected of being the bushrangers, they proceeded through Bindoon and on to New Norcia. When news of Joe's true whereabouts broke in Newcastle they were beyond recall and continued searching through Gingin and back down the Brockman River, returning home too late to join in the chase to the eastward. During his fruitless search McAtee spent a total of forty-nine days in the saddle and averaged 32 kilometres per day. In his report he stated: 'never, during 12 years service in the police, have I seen cleverer tracking done than by those natives employed on this occasion. For miles have they tracked over rocks, the absconders never setting foot on soft ground and often wearing slippers made of raw skins.'

McAtee and his comrades had spared no effort in pursuing the bushrangers, yet they received no special commendation; it was all just part of the job.

Joe's luck held for over a week. Then on Friday 21 September he and his mates were sighted near Youndegin by a party of sandalwood cutters and natives who immediately informed Lieutenant James Turner in charge of Hunt's road-making party. Hayden, the police constable stationed at Youndegin, was apparently out on patrol at the time, so Turner sent his native Cowitch into York with the news.[12] Since no police were available there, Moye, the sergeant in charge of the York police station, rushed a message to Kelly at Newcastle. Cowan, resident magistrate at York, communicated with George Hampton, requesting instructions as to the disposal of the bushrangers should they be caught and brought into York. Hampton replied that the governor wanted 'Johns and Co. to be sent direct to Fremantle so secured with irons etc. as to render escape impossible'.[13]

When the news reached Newcastle there were no police available there either, so Kelly sent a note out by the mail cart to be given to the first policeman met with. He then entrusted a local man with the task of locating Subinspector Piesse in the Avon valley, but the man returned the following morning stating that the police were nowhere to be found and that he had knocked up his horse in the attempt.[14] Kelly then borrowed the resident magistrate's pony, put pensioner Griffin in charge of the lockup and galloped off to see for himself. Near Bailup he met Constable Wheeler and Special Constable Holloway returning from escort duty. He persuaded Mr Martin to loan his horse and native to accompany Wheeler in search of Piesse and then returned to Newcastle. Wheeler finally came up with Piesse near Moondyne Spring on the 24th and the police party hastened back to Newcastle.[15]

That same day, a Monday, one of Joe's false leads was given to the police at Fremantle, but it came too late to be of any use to him. The following report was submitted by Sergeant Regan of Fremantle [*verb. et lit.*]:

> I beg leave to report for the information of the Superintendent that a man named Thomas Brown C.P. came to this station this day and reported that he met Moondine Joe a near Warren's, Gingin Road, about 10.00 p.m. on Friday night last and that either two or three men were

with him, all mounted, and that Johns gave him a soverin to get a bottle
of grog for him at Warren's which he did and that Johns treated him to
a part of the grog and told him that he was Moondine Joe and if he
would see any one looking for him to say that he met him.[16]

Since Joe was sighted near Youndegin on that day, either Brown
was lying for him or a group of Joe's friends had set Brown up by
masquerading as the bushrangers. Meanwhile, at York, Sergeant
Moye had sent Constable Edwards and a tracker out after the bushrangers. He had also hired a horse for 7*d* a day and mounted
another of his men, Constable Nugent, to accompany Edwards.
This was a temporary measure at best as both constables were
subpoenaed to appear at the next quarter sessions at the end of the
week, but Moye made sure that his officers would be well equipped.
He obtained an order from Resident Magistrate Cowan to Lieutenant Turner at Youndegin to detach one of his pensioner guards
and a native to accompany the police and to supply the party with
fresh horses and rations. Turner complied and the police party
moved on, strengthened by the addition of Peter Moore and Cowitch.

Back at Newcastle Piesse had returned to the police station with
Constables Hyde, Lally and Wheeler, and plans were being made
for Kelly to take a party out in pursuit of the bushrangers. Piesse,
being required to attend the quarter sessions and not knowing the
country to the eastward, was not going himself and had elected to
look after the police station until McAtee should return. A native
who knew the country was obtained to assist Kelly's party, which
consisted of Constables Lally, Wheeler and Monaghan and their
trackers, none of whom were required at the quarter sessions. All
eight men were mounted and they had a pack-horse to carry rations.
Kelly had no doubts about Joe's intentions towards Hunt's exploring   .
party, so the police under his command clattered out of Newcastle
at 11.00 am on Tuesday 25 September, bent on making the best
possible speed to Youndegin to pick up the trail.

The following afternoon Edwards and Nugent returned to York
with the information that Constable Hayden had found the bushrangers' tracks nearly 160 kilometres east of York. Hayden, Moore
and four trackers, all mounted and armed, were still on the trail.
Kelly heard this news when he passed through Youndegin and he
and his party pressed on with all speed.

12 Mounted Constables Haliday, Carmody and Edwards in the police uniforms of the 1860s, blue coats and brown trousers. Thomas Edwards was involved in the chase after Joe in September 1866.

The *Perth Gazette*, commenting on the possibility of Joe's capture, stated: 'we may shortly expect to hear of his capture or death, the latter however we do not think probable. Joe is too wide awake to show fight.'[17] The whole colony waited expectantly for news from the interior and conflicting rumours were rife. A Guildford correspondent to the *Inquirer* heard that the 'notorious Joe' had been secured but stated that he did not believe it. 'Old birds like he are not to be caught so easily', he said.[18]

This time nevertheless the rumour was true.

Hayden and his party had caught up with the bushrangers about midday on Saturday 29 September at Boodalin Soak, about 6 kilometres north-west of where Westonia townsite now stands.[19] They came upon Thomas Bugg first. He was lying in the shade of a bush resting, but as soon as Roser's dog began barking, he jumped up, grabbed his gun and was in the act of cocking it when Hayden fired at him. The ball passed through Bugg's right arm and grazed his breast. It was afterwards found inside his shirt completely flattened out. Joe and John James were found some distance away; they made no resistance whatsoever.

Later that afternoon Kelly's party arrived on the scene, having been delayed by one of their horses knocking up. Kelly, although disappointed at having missed out on the capture, was exultant that the men who had caused him so much trouble were finally in custody. The police dressed Bugg's arm and mounted him on the pack-horse for the return journey to York, but Joe and John James had to walk. Kelly commented that the prisoners seemed very angry at being caught, and certainly Joe would have been seething at this ignominious end to his plans.

It took a full week for the three prisoners and their fourteen triumphant guards to reach York. Once there, Kelly wished to take the gang across to Newcastle in order to lay charges, but Governor Hampton's orders prevailed. After a day's rest a cart was obtained and, with an escort of four constables and one native assistant led by Sergeant Kelly, the heavily-ironed prisoners were conveyed at full speed to the Convict Establishment. They arrived there at 3.00 am on Tuesday 9 October.

Kelly's report states that Joe and John James fired upon a native woman and boy near Youndegin but, both guns misfiring, the natives

13 The old Youndegin police station

14 Hunt's Well at Boodalin Soak, where Joe, Bugg and James were captured on 29 September 1866

got away. He intended to have the natives conveyed to York and the matter brought to the attention of the resident magistrate, yet nothing ever came of it. It is not hard to believe that the bushrangers should have tried to prevent news of their whereabouts getting back to York, but that both guns should misfire, one in the hands of a bushman of Joe's experience, seems incredible. Resident Magistrate Cowan, however, was still sympathetic towards Joe. Although he recommended liberal rewards to Hayden, Moore and the four native assistants who participated in the capture, he also spoke with Joe and wrote to George Hampton, suggesting Joe's innocence and requesting to see the original deposition regarding his case. The acting comptroller-general replied that he did not agree and that he considered Joe 'an immense scoundrel'.[20]

The first sight which met the eyes of the chain-gang when they left their cells on Tuesday morning was Joe chained by the neck to the iron bar of a window in the prison yard. A cheeky piece in the *Perth Gazette* lampooned the governor's relief.

> Gossip says that His Excellency became painfully prostrated after reading his despatches on Tuesday and spiritual assistance was obliged to be resorted to. Change of scene being considered advisable His Excellency proceeded to Fremantle and took a refreshing sight at "Moondyne Joe" chained to a post in a yard in the Convict Establishment, after which he was able to return to Perth with his mind in its normal state of placidity. It is not said whether the "spiritual assistance" referred to was the prayers and blessings of the Clergy.[21]

The governor was indeed happy to have Joe in custody again, and he intended to make absolutely certain that Joe made no further escapes. But Joe was to prove equally determined.

REFERENCES

1. *Perth Gazette* 14, 28 September 1866.
2. Police Records, WAA Acc. No. 422, vol. 2.
3. Ibid Acc. No. 129 9/778.
4. *Perth Gazette* 12 October 1866.
5. Police Records, WAA Acc. No. 422, vol. 2.
6. Ibid Acc. No. 129 9/802.

7. Ibid 9/778.
8. Ibid Acc. No. 422, vol. 2.
9. Ibid Acc. No. 129 9/802.
10. Ibid Acc. No. 422, vol. 2.
11. Ibid Acc. No. 129 9/802.
12. Ibid Acc. No. 371 5.
13. Convict Records, WAA Acc. No. 1156 C50-7573.
14. Police Records, WAA Acc. No. 422, vol. 2.
15. Ibid Acc. No. 129 9/802.
16. Ibid.
17. *Perth Gazette* 28 September 1866.
18. *Inquirer* 10 October 1866.
19. Police Records, WAA Acc. No. 129 9/802; *Perth Gazette* 12 October 1866.
20. Convict Records, WAA Acc. No. 1156 C50-7573.
21. *Perth Gazette* 12 October 1866.

Chapter nine

1866-1867

Joe's new quarters were not exactly comfortable. Within four days
Dr Attfield, the prison surgeon, reported that insufficient ventilation
was affecting the prisoner's health. After due consideration by the
acting comptroller-general a pane of glass was removed from the
cell window: Joe breathed a little easier.[1] The following week he was
sentenced to further time behind bars and his case prompted editorial
comment from the *Perth Gazette*:

> As the law with respect to escaped prisoners now stands, where no
> personal injury is actually inflicted, its application is a mere farce so
> far as punishment can be inflicted, especially when it is viewed as it
> should be—as a means to deter the criminal and others of his class
> from again committing a little offence. What can possibly be the use
> of heaping sentence after sentence of penal servitude upon men whose
> freedom has already been forfeited by sentences that cannot possibly
> be carried out within the usual duration of human life. A notable
> instance of the light in which this is viewed by the convicts themselves,
> was furnished a few days since, when a notorious convict named Johns
> who has twice made his escape and taken to the bush, and during the

freedom so obtained, committed numberless robberies upon the
settlers. For his last escapade of this kind he was last week arraigned
before the Fremantle Bench, when he was sentenced to 2 years hard
labour for the escape and 3 for the robberies and he then told the
magistrate he might sentence him to 40 years if he liked.[2]

The futility of long sentences as a deterrent was not recognized by
others. In fact the police had been expressly requested to present
the case of robbery because the maximum sentence for absconding
was not considered sufficient punishment for Joe.[3] Everett and Roser,
who appeared as witnesses for the prosecution and identified the
goods stolen from them (see Appendix C), had all their expenses
paid from colonial funds, and the resident magistrate of Fremantle
was informed by George Hampton that the governor himself desired
a case of robbery if at all possible.[4] Strangely the bushrangers were
never tried for the robbery at Dodd's despite a strongly worded note
from Sergeant Kelly pointing out that more violence was used in
Dodd's case than any other robbery committed by them.[5] At the
completion of the court proceedings the new resident magistrate of
Newcastle, William John Clifton, wrote to the colonial secretary
asking why Joe had not been tried for the robbery at Dodd's since
this involved 'more serious consequences than the robberies at
Everett's and Roser's.' The letter was referred to the acting
comptroller-general, George Hampton, who was against a further
trial and stated: 'the men could not be in a worse position practically,
than they are at present.'[6] Only a few days previously Hampton had
almost lost his life at the Fremantle quarries when a convict named
Connor had attacked him with a pickaxe. Only the swift action of
one of the guards, a Corporal Clayton, had saved him.[7] Perhaps
this unnerving experience prompted a little leniency.

In the meantime a very special cell was being prepared to house
Joe and make all chance of another escape impossible.[8] Under the
supervision of H. Jarvis of the Colonial Works Office, the stone
walls of a second-floor cell were rebuilt and the interior completely
lined with heavy sleepers. These were fastened to the stone walls
with hundreds of heavy dog spikes and a strong mesh grille was
fitted over the tiny barred window. The cell was guaranteed escape-
proof but was also almost air-proof and light-proof. Joe was hustled
into it and put on a diet of bread and water as a disciplinary

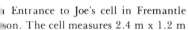

15b

15c

a Entrance to Joe's cell in Fremantle ~~Pri~~son. The cell measures 2.4 m x 1.2 m

b Rear wall and triple-barred window of Joe's cell

c Interior of Joe's cell showing door ~~and~~ heavy timbers fastened to the walls with iron dog spikes

measure. The usual hammock hooks were removed and presumably Joe slept on the floor. There had been some talk of driving a ring bolt into the floor of the cell and chaining the prisoner to it as an extra precaution but Hampton decided that this measure was unnecessary.[9]

Joe's companions fared only slightly better. John James was set to hard labour in the chain-gang, while Thomas Bugg recuperated from his wound in solitary confinement before joining him. Bassett who had been in solitary on bread and water ever since his capture, was now included in an outside chain-gang.[10] Evans, Joe's companion on his former escape, was still in irons, and despite repeated petitions his behaviour was considered too violent for release. His irons were struck off in February 1867.[11] John James never regained his freedom. He died in the prison hospital in April 1872. Bassett was set free in May 1872, but Bugg remained in prison until 1885.[12]

After only two weeks in his cramped quarters Joe's health began to fail and Dr Attfield reported his unfitness for further bread-and-water treatment. By the time a month was up Attfield advised that it was dangerous to keep the prisoner in his present cell any longer. Joe's exercise period was doubled to two hours daily and the ventilation in his cell was improved,[13] but Acting Comptroller-General Hampton was reluctant to abandon the use of his masterpiece, the cell supreme.

Early in 1867 Joe's poor health prompted the authorities to employ him on open-air labour during daylight hours, but this was only done under extremely strict conditions. He was not let out of his cell until after all the other convicts had gone to their various places of employment. Joe was put to the interesting work of breaking stones, but rather than take him outside the prison to the stones, each morning a quantity of stones was wheeled into the prison yard and dumped near the wall ready for him to work on. He worked under the constant supervision of a sentry, and prison officers were also directed to visit him at frequent intervals. He could not leave certain limits for any purpose unless accompanied by the sentry and no other convicts were allowed to approach within 18 metres of Joe's working place. Each evening, after Joe was safely locked away again, the results of his labours were to be removed.[14]

Under such conditions escape was impossible but Joe did not lose heart. In fact his heart leapt when he noticed the failure of prison officials to observe one of the conditions: the broken rock was not being taken away; it was slowly but surely growing into a substantial heap. This oversight was to give Joe the opportunity for his most spectacular escape. Yet in spite of his exultation he forced himself to remain calm and work slowly, stopping for frequent rest periods as befitted his supposed poor health.

The days passed monotonously, the warder's vigilance relaxed and still the heap of broken stones continued to grow. Eventually there were periods when Joe's body below his waist was obscured from the view of his bored guard. Only then, when he was certain to escape detection, did Joe take his first experimental swing at the thick prison wall. The limestone crumbling under his sledge-hammer must have been a wonderful sight to Joe, but again he was careful to give no outward sign of his elation.

We shall never know just how long it took him to break a hole in the wall large enough for his exit. Then suddenly at 5.00 pm on March 7 the signal gun at the prison was fired: a convict named Thomas Morris had escaped from the Fremantle Bridge chain-gang.[15] An immediate check on Joe was made but it was too late: he was gone. Within hours the towns of Fremantle and Perth were buzzing with the news. An article in the *Perth Gazette* conveys the various reactions to his disappearance.

> Probably no event in the colony ever more tickled the risible faculties of the public than the escape of the notorious convict, Moondyne Joe, on the afternoon of Thursday last week. Much of the amusement felt arose from remembrance of the theatrical exhibition made of Joe by the Acting Comptroller General when he was last captured — chaining him to a post in one of the yards and Mr. Hampton improving the occasion by addressing the assembled prisoners and pointing out to them Joe's sad condition as an example of what would befall them if they went and did likewise.
>
> Joe's ingenuity in making his escape from his apparently hopeless condition has gained him many sympathisers who express an opinion that he has earned his freedom, more especially as Mr. Hampton is said to have told him, when he saw him put into the cell which had been specially prepared for him, that if he managed to make his escape again, he would forgive him. That cell was made wonderfully strong, as much so as iron and wood could make it . . . The Surgeon

however, reported that a greater amount of open air was necessary for the maintenance of health, consequently Mr. Hampton selected a position in the angle of the wall at the back of the yard of the Superintendent's house and there Joe was set to work at stone breaking under the eye of the sentry upon the prison walls and the warder of the chain gang working in the yard. How long he was so employed we know not, but on Thursday afternoon on being visited by the warder, the prisoner was gone and in his place was a neatly contrived dummy. It seems that the broken stone had been allowed to accumulate until it got to a considerable height and, together with that unbroken which Joe had been allowed to pile around him, concealed his person below the waist from the view of the sentry and the warder, a chance which Joe did not allow to escape; his plan must have taken some time to execute for the first thing was to provide a means of getting through the wall, a work of considerable labour, and the progress of which it was necessary to hide from his visitors by making it assume its usual appearance as the time for each periodical visit approached. The hole ready through the wall into Mr. Lefroy's yard, Joe then prepared for his exit by sticking his hammer upright and, with some umbrella wire he had got possession of, he formed a shape something of a man's shoulders and arms; upon the top he placed his cap, and having split up the sleeves of his jacket and shirt, managed to slip out of them and leave them on the frame he had constructed, then, having got rid of his irons and divested himself of his trowsers [*sic*], got through his hole in the wall, passed through Mr. Lefroy's yard and out at a side door to the front of the prison, whence to a person of Joe's practised sagacity a safe transit to the neighbouring bush became an easy matter.

When the escape was discovered the consternation amongst the prison officials is said to have been something worth witnessing; the warder who did not ascertain the fact until he had actually taken the dummy by the arm was nearly sick with fright; the Superintendent could not believe it and brought forward a theory that it could not possibly be a fact.

However the alarm bell was rung, the gun was fired and the police and the military distributed and an express sent to Perth, which is said to have greatly disturbed His Excellency and Mr. Hampton's digestion of their dinner and did not greatly contribute to their repose during the night or the day after.[16]

The first policemen on the scene were Subinspector William Snook and Constable Pollard of Fremantle. Snook reported droves of pensioner guards and others searching the bush in the neighbourhood of the prison. Some tracks were got, he stated, of two men supposed to be those of Joe and Morris. They were tracked in the direction of Mr Wellard's piggery but further attempts at pursuit had to await daylight the following morning. Snook suggested that some mounted men be sent to the Canning district as he felt that the absconders would be certain to head for the hills.[17]

The Perth police were not long in taking this action. That evening Sergeant W. Dale drew up a detailed set of orders for all the officers he could spare.

> P.C. Jackaman and nat. asst. — Will proceed at once to the lower Canning bridge and remain concealed in such a manner that he has a command of all persons crossing or passing up the river during the night. To keep a sharp lookout for the above mentioned absconders *who are to be taken dead or alive* [author's italics]. He will be relieved at daylight by M.C. Campbell who, with the native assistant will proceed up the direction of Bull's Creek to the Upper Canning.
>
> P.C. Buck and assistant — To the Canning with despatch and to prosecute the search for the absconders in conjunction with P.C. Dunmall. A sharp lookout to be kept tonight; the same orders as to their capture given as above.
>
> P.C. Campbell — To Guildford with despatch notifying their escape and to order Sergeant Peacock to send a Mounted Constable and native to Wanneroo at once.
>
> A. S. Bentley — To the Causeway Bridge on duty until daylight.
>
> P.C. Kennedy — To patrol the suburbs in Ranford's direction.
>
> P.C. Maloney — To patrol the upper parts of Perth.
>
> P.C. McCamish — To patrol under Mt. Eliza as far as the block road.
>
> P.C. Campbell and assistant — To Bull's Creek and elsewhere in search.
>
> Corpl. Furlong and assistant — To Butler's Swamp, thence to Wanneroo in search of the absconders; the same orders given as in the first mentioned respecting their capture.[18]

So before Joe, cutting a ridiculous figure in his boots and underclothes, could have got far, police stations in a wide semi-circle between Fremantle and the hills had been alerted. For the first time in the history of the Western Australian convict era, orders had been given to take an absconder dead or alive. It was rumoured that

16 Memorandum from Sergeant Dale of Perth,
ordering extreme measures to be taken to facili-
tate Joe's capture

George Hampton had offered a reward of £20 from his private purse
if Joe's body could be brought in the following day,[19] but no such
offer was ever made officially.

The police were on the move at dawn and by that evening Thomas
Morris had been captured.[20] Although an incredible coincidence, it
is doubtful that the escape of Morris was in any way connected with
Joe's. Such timing would have been virtually impossible to achieve,
and the slightest slip could have ruined Joe's chances. In fact the
escape of Morris caused the hole in the wall to be discovered much
earlier than Joe would have hoped.

By the second day of the hunt nearly twenty mounted police and
trackers were actively searching the coastal plain for Joe, while
diligent enquiry was made within the towns by constables on foot.[21]
The news was on the way to all the scattered farming centres, where
police were urged to keep a sharp lookout, and before long, heads
were being shaken throughout the colony at Joe's colossal impudence.

The only police with a real lead were Sergeant Regan and Cor-

Perth 7 March 1867

652, Thomas Jones has made his escape from Gang this evening &

fg Joseph B John's from the Fremantle prison

... at once to the lower Canning bridge and concealed in such a manner that he has a command over crossing or passing up the River during the night keep look out for the above mentioned Absconders be taken dead or alive he will be relieved at day Campbell who with the native Assistant will ... the direction of Bulls Creek, to the Upper Canning ... with despatch and to prosecute the search

poral Ryan of Fremantle who followed up the tracks noticed by Snook near the prison. The tracks petered out at Wungong but fresh ones were found leading away from there three days later. These were followed into the hills, where they were soon lost in the rugged country east of Wungong. It was never proved that these tracks were actually Joe's, and Regan and Ryan were to spend a further two weeks searching fruitlessly through Wandering and out to the east of Beverley before returning to their station. Constables Armstrong and Pollard, also from Fremantle, who spent ten days searching through the Murray district and across the hills to Williams, were equally unsuccessful. Constables Dunmall and Campbell kept up a continual search of the Canning district and the hills between Greenmount and Ben Mason's timber station. They also made several excursions up the Helena valley but found no trace of the elusive Joe. In Guildford Constable Woodbridge had been left in charge, while Sergeant Peacock and Constable Allely headed south and Constable McAtee and his Tracker Johnny headed north.

Although the countryside was now swarming with various police parties, it was also alive with rumours which were a great hindrance to the police. At Wanneroo McAtee, who had joined forces with Corporal Furlong, questioned Mr James Cowle, a surveyor, at his camp. Cowle informed him that on the second night after the escape his dogs had kept up a continual and unusual barking and that he had found the tracks of a white man nearby in the morning. The lead came to nothing but McAtee did not return empty-handed. In scouring the hills around Moondyne Spring a few days later he captured an absconder named John Brown who was arrested and marched into Guildford.

Sergeant Peacock, who had searched southwards as far as William Foster's Narrogin Inn and returned along the hills to the York road, decided to question the settlers along the base of the hills. He stated:

> On our arriving at Mr. Smith's on the Helena we were there informed by Mrs. Smith that her husband told her a man named Mr. Summers on the Swan saw a man on the Perth Road on the 8th inst. very much resembling the appearance of Moondyne Joe and most likely it might have been him. We at once proceeded to Mr. Summers' on the Swan and, when arrived there at 7.00 p.m., he informed us that he had seen a man but could not tell who he was or whether it had been the escaped convict or no. He also stated that he heard of a man being taken in Guildford and locked up for committing a robbery. I then thought it would be better for me to make sure who the man was. I therefore proceeded to Guildford and there found that the man which had been locked up was a T.L. named Stuart for stealing some onions from the Govt. Garden in Perth.[22]

This was a frustrating waste of time and Peacock decided to extend his search along the Swan and up the Avon.

In the meantime the following report was submitted by Constable Albert Woodbridge.

> I beg respectfully to report for the information of the Superintendent of Police that Warder Hollis of Guildford Depot brought to Station at half past eight a.m. the 10th inst. a report that Asst. Warder Sinclair's house at the four mile camp York Road had been broken open during the night and some things taken away. At 10.00 a.m. P.C. Moore and Native Assistant left Station for Warder Sinclair's

Party and returned to Station at 6 p.m. reporting that about 30 lbs. of Bread and 4 lbs. of Meat had been stolen from Warder Sinclair's house between the hours of 12 and 1½ Midnight. P.C. Moore reports that there was no proper fastening on the door and anyone knowing the place might open it as easy as any ordinary door. The native was unable to find any tracks leading to or from the Camp or any traces of the robbery. Warder Sinclair reports that a cap and handkerchief was stolen from one of the prisoners during the night. The bread and meat was the property of Warder Sinclair.[23]

Mr Crampton, the acting superintendent of police, thought it possible that the robbery was committed by Joe because of his having left his cap behind him at the prison, but no further information came to light and the matter was forgotten.

Up at Newcastle Sergeant Kelly had his doubts that Joe would risk a return to his old haunts but, just in case, he had a man named John Holloway sworn in as a Special Constable. Holloway was rigged out in the clothes of a bushman, armed with a double-barrelled gun and ordered to patrol the road between Bailup and Penifather's place, keeping himself well hidden. Kelly considered that Joe, being ignorant of his old mate's treachery, might call at Penifather's for assistance. The plan nevertheless was doomed to failure. Holloway was spotted lurking in the bush at the roadside by several night travellers including the mailman. Since he made off without speaking whenever he was seen, suspicion ran high and, as Kelly ruefully reported, 'every body has it in their mouth that it is Moondine Jo.' When Sergeant Peacock arrived at Bailup he was informed of the presence of this suspicious gentleman of the road and spent three days tracking Kelly's special constable. The local wags had many a laugh at the expense of the police over that episode, but the real laugh was on Governor Hampton and his son, the acting comptroller-general.

On Monday the 11th these two dignitaries arrived in Fremantle to enquire into Joe's escape and who was to blame for it.[24] Joe's warder, a man named Cook, had been blamed by the prison superintendent, while in return Cook stated that the superintendent's opinion was affected by personal malice. After the enquiry Cook was docked four days' pay and allowances and his exertion money was stopped, even though the *Inquirer* stated that he was acquitted of neglect of duty.[25] That newspaper also reported that the officers who were to blame would have to pay the whole expense involved in the pursuit out of their own pockets,[26] but this would have been an enormous sum and apparently no such action was ever taken. The public in general were not concerned with apportioning blame. The governor and his son were laughing-stocks and people were intent on enjoying the joke. A rhyme went round which was chanted to the tune of a well-known air.

> The Governor's son has got the pip,
> The Governor's got the measles.
> But Moondyne Joe has give 'em the slip.
> Pop goes the weasel.

This irritating little tune was sung and whistled by all the urchins in Perth and did nothing to restore the governor's good humour.[27]

Gradually the police search ground to a halt. No tracks could be found, and although sightings and thefts were reported spasmodically, most were found to be groundless. One rumour had it that Joe was concealed at Point Walter, however a thorough search of the area failed to flush him out. He was supposedly seen at Bindoon and in the Moondyne hills, yet searches of these areas were also fruitless.[28] The orders of the governor and his son to take Joe dead or alive had not helped. As the *Perth Gazette* put it, 'this kind consideration of Mr. Hampton for Joe's health was not productive of benefit to either for the latter is still enjoying his liberty, and has completely vanished without leaving tracks.'[29]

A month passed and still nothing had been heard of Joe. Then Subinspector Piesse reported that Joe had been seen near where the Swan River emerges from the hills 'and that a plant was found by a native in the River yesterday, and that tracks of a man with muffled feet was seen by the native at the spot and quite fresh.'[30] As this certainly sounded like Joe, Constable Allely with Native Assistant George were sent out to investigate. They found nothing and that was the last really good lead that the police were to get for some considerable time.

Nearly three weeks later the *Perth Gazette* reported: 'Nothing has yet been heard of the notorious Moondyne Joe who is probably harboured by some of his sympathisers in the bush, as he has committed no robberies of rations for his support.'[31] There can be little doubt that this theory was correct. Joe could not have eluded the massive police manhunt without a great deal of help. Somebody gave him clothing soon after he escaped as he could not have got far in his underclothes. No clothing, apart from a cap, was reported stolen. It is possible that a continuance of active police search and enquiry may have resulted in Joe's capture, but subsequent events were to keep the police so busy that Joe was all but forgotten.

REFERENCES

1. Convict Records, WAA Acc. No. 1156 C50-7573.
2. *Perth Gazette* 26 October 1866.
3. Comptroller General to Colonial Secretary, 1 November 1866, WAA CS0583.
4. Convict Records, WAA Acc. No. 1156 C50-7573.
5. Police Records, WAA Acc. No. 129 9/912.
6. Resident Magistrate of Newcastle to Colonial Secretary, 29 October 1866, WAA CS0583.
7. Governor's Correspondence, 25 October 1866, WAA Acc. No. 136.
8. Convict Records, WAA Acc. No. 1156 C32-164.
9. Ibid C50-7573.
10. Ibid.
11. Ibid C48-6072.
12. Ibid R21B.
13. Ibid C50-7573.
14. *Inquirer* 13 March 1867.
15. Convict Records, WAA Acc. No. 1156 C50-8730.
16. *Perth Gazette* 15 March 1867.
17. Police Records, WAA Acc. No. 129 10/463.
18. Ibid.
19. *Perth Gazette* 15 March 1867.
20. Convict Records, WAA Acc. No. 1156 C50-8730.
21. Police Records, WAA Acc. No. 129 10/463.
22. Ibid.
23. Ibid.
24. *Inquirer* 13 March 1867.
25. Convict Records, WAA Acc. No. 1156 C50-8730.
26. *Inquirer* 13 March 1867.
27. *Sunday Times* 27 May 1928.

28. Police Records, WAA Acc. No. 129 10/463.
29. *Perth Gazette* 15 March 1867.
30. Police Records, WAA Acc. No. 129 10/463.
31. *Perth Gazette* 26 April 1867.

Chapter ten

1867-1869

There can be no doubt that for some time Joe's spectacular escape was the main topic of conversation amongst the inmates of Fremantle Prison. His success set many of the other prisoners to working out ways and means of emulating him. In fact only two days after Joe's escape a convict at the Fremantle Lunatic Asylum construction works bolted, taking advantage of the almost complete absence of mounted police who were all out in pursuit of Joe.[1] A week later two of the stringent-discipline class, Mason and Morrill, made their escape. They were disturbed while attempting to break into Mr Saw's store at Guildford, but managed to steal a gun each from one of the homesteads further up the river. Soon afterwards they were sighted on the Upper Swan bridge, where in sheer bravado they fired off three shots. On the same evening they held up the warden in charge of a party of probationers near Warren's Bush Inn, and that night, stole a horse each and two bottles of grog from a dray parked outside the inn. One of the horses was Warren's, while the other belonged to a team from the New Norcia Mission and the

99

monk in charge, Brother John, gave chase. Drawing alongside one of the would-be bushrangers he sternly demanded the return of his horse. The absconder took one look at him, leapt from the horse and took to his heels. Having recovered one horse, Brother John decided that he might as well try for the other. The result was the same and the monk was able to return to Warren's leading both horses before daylight.[2] Mason and Morrill were captured not long after this, but by then far more dangerous birds than these were planning to fly. Joe had been gone nearly three months when William Graham, under sentence for shooting Mr Quartermaine (see Chapter Four), succeeded in making a clean getaway from Fremantle Prison.[3] He was accompanied by two other convicts, Thomas Scott and George Morris, both ex sailors who had been transported for crimes of violence.

Scott had been sentenced to fourteen years for mutinous conduct and violence to his superior officer.[4] He had gained a conditional pardon in 1864 but was reconvicted for assault the following year. In 1866 he had absconded from the York depot. He was caught and returned to Fremantle where he had assaulted a warder.[5] Morris had got twenty years for wounding with intent. The latter was only twenty-one years old when he arrived in the colony in December 1865, but like Scott had been in continual trouble ever since. At the time of teaming up with Graham and Scott he was doing time in Fremantle Prison for assaulting a fellow prisoner at Guildford lockup and had just been unfettered after a four months' spell in irons.[6] Scott had served twelve months of an eighteen months' sentence.[7]

The escape took place during the stormy night of 29 May 1867.[8] All three prisoners were confined in the same ward but in separate tiers of cells. The ward was guarded by two warders who at intervals during the night had the duty of entering the cells containing prisoners in irons. It was while the guards were so engaged that Graham used a duplicate key to open his cell door, crept along the catwalks, the sound of his footsteps deadened by the pelting rain outside, and liberated his companions. Just how the key came into Graham's possession was never satisfactorily explained.

From the ward the three men had to pass directly under the bright lamps lighting the prison yard, which they did still undetected. They made their way silently to the prison workshop and spent some time cutting a strip of leather from one of the long belts supplying drive to the machines. This leather rope was used to assist them in scaling the wall.

The whole escape had been executed quickly and quietly and their absence was not detected until the next morning, when red faces were a feature of officialdom. The affair caused the governor and acting comptroller-general much embarrassment, but the attitude of the public differed greatly from when Joe had made his escape. Graham and his mates were considered dangerous and the colonists were alarmed and frightened.

The trio of escapees were not long in beginning bushranging activities to support themselves. After crossing the Fremantle Bridge they acquired a double-barrelled gun from John Atkinson's place near 'Butlers Swamp' (Lake Claremont), and on the morning of their second day of freedom they held up Scrivener's place near the 'Peninsula Farm' north east of Perth, providing themselves with food, another double-barrelled gun, ammunition and a watch. As soon as the news was heard in Perth the police rushed to the scene, but they had hardly begun following up the tracks when a report arrived that their quarry had just stuck up Oliver's house at Bassendean. The police immediately transferred their efforts to Oliver's and again began the work of tracking, however by this time it was nearly dark and they did not get far.

Meanwhile in Guildford measures were taken to prevent the fugitives from crossing the river. Guards were mounted in the town and the moorings of the residents' 'mosquito fleet' altered. Constables Armstrong and Kirk, with Trackers George and Sambo, were despatched across the river to work their way towards the Perth police. Before they left, Subinspector Piesse made it clear that they were in pursuit of dangerous and desperate men. At all costs the police were not to allow themselves to be killed. The advice was taken to heart as this newspaper report shows:

> The darkness prevented much progress being made, and the native dismounted and struck a match to enable him to search the ground for tracks, when one of the constables saw the three runaways a few yards ahead running under the boughs of a low and wide spreading gum tree, from whence a shot was immediately after fired; the police returned the fire and then heard the sound of men running away,

and attempted to follow, but the night was too dark to allow of their penetrating the bush on horseback. On searching under the tree they found the body of Morris, who had been shot with a ball from a revolver, passing into his neck and out of his back and beside the body was Mr. Scrivener's gun and several of the things stolen from Mr. Oliver.[9]

Reflecting the attitude of locals, a Guildford correspondent wrote:

It is to be regretted that after the encounter on Friday evening that all did not dismount as the aborigine did, and seize the remaining two while their guns were discharged; such an opportunity lost does no credit to our police force. Who is to blame in this affair I know not, but the warm reception the police got beyond Mr. Hammersley's flat seems to have cooled their courage; and beyond guarding the town I hear of nothing being done to catch them. Is it imagined that Graham will follow Joe's example and trouble no one?[10]

Opinions on the behaviour of the police during the fracas continued to be published for some weeks.[11] Nevertheless the continual heavy rain prevented much being done in the way of organized pursuit and Graham and Scott moved round the countryside with impunity.

On Sunday night they held up Joseph Inglis between Guildford and Perth and demanded his horse, but the plucky fellow dug in his heels and galloped away with the bushrangers' bullets whining past his ears. Next day they were seen on Kings Meadow at Guildford, and although the alarm was sounded and police, pensioners and volunteers shouldered arms and rushed to the spot, they again got away. That night they stopped a pensioner named McMahon and demanded to know how much money he had but let him go when it was found that he only had 1s 6d. Just after midnight on Wednesday night they burst into Mayo's house on the Upper Swan and demanded food. Mr and Mrs Mayo were reported to have dived out their bedroom window and spent the rest of the night in the bush, leaving their house to the tender mercies of the bushrangers who, of course, helped themselves. It was also reported that the mailman from Gingin had been stopped and the mail bags taken from him.

The *Perth Gazette* suggested that extreme measures were now required:

Of course the Police are in hot pursuit of these desperate characters, but the state of the weather almost precludes the possibility of tracking them as their tracks are washed out almost as soon as made. There is but one measure which will rid the country of them and that is the issue of a proclamation offering a sufficient reward for their bodies dead or alive; such a procedure is undoubtedly shocking to contemplate, but on the other hand we have to consider the men we have to deal with, their evident determination to stick at nothing in their desperate course, and the danger in which, not only the property, but the lives of the settlers are placed by their being at large; it is manifestly the duty of the Government to do the utmost to rid the colony of such men and to allay the alarm now existing.[12]

Later it was found that they had doubled back down the river, crossed near the Causeway and headed east by way of the Canning River. They made their presence known at Beverley by robbing a shepherd's hut and calling at Wansborough's place for provisions, but still the police did not succeed in catching them.[13] They were thought to be heading eastwards and all was quiet for a few weeks. People were just beginning to calm down when one of the most daring and sensational mass escapes ever made from Fremantle Prison took place.

The ringleaders were John Williams and Bernard Woottan. Both had made two previous escapes and tasted the bushranging life (see Chapters Four and Six) and were considered determined and dangerous. With them went William Watkins, Walter Walker, J. Slim, W. Stuart, R. O'Locklin, E. Onions and J. Billings.[14] The escape was described in the *Perth Gazette* as follows:

On the evening of the 8th of August, shortly after the working gangs of convicts had been marched into prison for the night, the door of one of the wards was opened and from it emerged a party of eight men apparently under the charge of a man in a warder's uniform; he halted his party while he reclosed and locked the door, and then giving the order to march took them to the gate of the work yard, passing on the way a sentry just relieved, who seeing the apparent warder took no notice of the party. Unlocking the workshop yard gate and passing through it, it was re-locked, and the fellows having barricaded it were secure from observation; they then raised two ladders against the outer wall of the prison, and with ropes fastened to the upper rounds quickly let themselves down the other side.[15]

The party was sighted by a warder who lived nearby, but although the alarm was given immediately, darkness and rain again prevented any effectual pursuit. The escapees were not long in resorting to bushranging tactics, and in the course of robbing Hay's place near Rockingham started a fire which completely gutted the building. A few days later seven of them were sighted at Dandalup and Constable Thomas Keen of Pinjarra and his Native Assistant Billy Murray went out in pursuit. Four of the escapees surrendered immediately but the remainder took to their heels. Keen waited until assistance arrived and then galloped off after them. Two of the runaways, Slim and Walker, managed to get away but Billy Murray caught up with Watkins who produced a pistol and fired wildly. No one was hit, and when Keen caught up, Watkins was taken. He was later, after an interesting trial, found not guilty of attempting to shoot Billy Murray.[16]

Through the whole mêlée there was no sign of Williams or Woottan, though it is unlikely that they were far away. Later events prove that they were joined by Slim and Walker soon after the brush with the police. Williams was keen on attempting another escape by ship, whereas Woottan preferred an overland attempt. Eventually they decided to split up, Woottan and Walker heading east and Williams and Slim towards the ports of Bunbury and Busselton.

At that time speculation on the whereabouts of William Graham and Thomas Scott gave that pair a good chance of making it to South Australia. The press reported that 'the principal obstacle usually prevailing against an overland route — want of water — has been, it is supposed, obviated by the heavy and long continued falls of rain which have occurred along the whole range of the south coast.'[17]

Considering the watch that would have been put on the ports, Woottan and Walker probably made the most intelligent choice; nevertheless they were captured within days by Constable Edward Barron at Seabrook's place near Beverley.

Barron was joined by Sergeant Moye and together they escorted the prisoners to York. The party stayed overnight at the home of William Chadwicke, where the prisoners were handcuffed together and provided with a rug to sleep in. About 2.00 am they asked to have one hand released to enable them to turn over, so Moye handcuffed them separately and went back to bed. At breakfast Woottan complained that he could not eat unless his right hand was released, and the trusting sergeant, impressed by his good behaviour, released him. With breakfast over, Barron and Moye knelt on the floor to roll up the prisoners' rug when Woottan showed his true colours. Seizing a red-hot iron bar from the fireplace he bashed Moye over the head with it. Moye, although badly hurt, staggered to his feet and was promptly struck again and knocked down. Both Barron and Native Assistant Jack Bousher leapt into the fray and finally Woottan was subdued and handcuffed. Holding his head, which was bleeding profusely, Moye asked the prisoner why he had attacked him. Woottan, whose hands were badly burnt from holding the iron bar, replied: 'Would you not have done it to get your liberty?'

Woottan was later found guilty of attempted murder and sentenced to death. After his execution the press reported: 'this man was undoubtedly one of the most desperate and dangerous characters we have been indebted for to the mother country.'[18] He continued hardened to the last, rejecting all offers of religious ministrations and his last words were a shout for the Irish republic.

Not long after the capture of Woottan and Walker, Slim was caught in the Murray district. John Williams was never caught. Slim reported that his companion had been drowned swimming the flooded Murray River, but the police ridiculed his statement, after they had found and followed two sets of tracks for 16 kilometres south of the river.[19] Just whose tracks these were remains a mystery because Slim's statement was later proved correct by the discovery of Williams's body.[20]

While all this excitement was going on, a party of four police and three natives were doggedly following the tracks of William Graham and Thomas Scott. After reaching the south coast they had returned north-west toward the more settled districts. At length the police found fresh tracks about 105 kilometres east of Kojonup, at the edge of some thick scrub, and it was obvious that the two outlaws were concealed close at hand. The police made camp and sent the native trackers to reconnoitre. After some search the trackers sighted a fire, the light of which flickered on a rough hut and outlined Graham doing sentry duty in the doorway. Returning to the police camp in pitch darkness, the trackers reported their discovery, and the police after some consultation came to a decision which was

later said to have 'cast shame on the whole force'. Apparently the
trackers were ordered to return and watch the hut until Graham
retired inside, and then to fire on the building without challenge.
The natives obeyed these orders literally and then immediately
returned to the police camp, leaving the occupants of the hut to die
or escape as chance may have directed their fire. The morning light
showed that both bushrangers had escaped, although not unscathed.
On the following day Graham, badly wounded in the right arm and
foot, gave himself up to a shepherd, having managed to drag himself some 19 kilometres from the scene of the shoot-out. Scott was
captured a few days later near the Blackwood River. It was afterwards reported that the police concerned in the 'disgraceful affair'
had been dismissed from the force.[21]

Despite the shadow cast on the police force by this affair, the
press were pleased to announce that 'the colony [was] again able to
rejoice in its freedom from any marauding by escaped convicts!' It
appears that Joe had been completely forgotten. His freedom from
pursuit was apparently due to the lack of marauding undertaken by
him. One can only speculate as to where he hid and how he lived
during this period. Since game was plentiful in his favourite haunt,
the wild country along the Avon valley, with Joe's knowledge of the
bush, survival would not have been difficult. The hills abounded
with kangaroos and wallabies and, if Joe had the use of a gun, fresh
meat would have been easy to come by. One animal that Joe would
have been unable to include on his menu was the rabbit. These
animals were not common in Western Australia until they staged
the massive migration in 1894 that led to the construction of the
longest fence in the world, the Number One Rabbit-Proof Fence.
But other animals were available and even the lack of a gun would
have been no great drawback. For instance, once a tree containing
a possum was found, the animal could be easily snared by leaning a
pole against the trunk of the tree. Possums prefer to descend a tree
by the easiest route and a wire noose set on the sloping pole will
rarely fail to strangle the animal. Suitably-baited traps in the deeper
pools along the river would ensure a supply of the freshwater catfish
or cobbler, and small freshwater crustaceans called gilgies could be
lured to the surface by baits and scooped up in a 'billy'. The river
pools were frequented by numerous wildfowl which too could be

snared soundlessly. A tempting morsal would be attached by string to a heavy rock which would be then balanced on the tip of a stake driven into the river bed. When an unwary bird swallowed the bait and attempted to paddle away, the rock would topple off the stake pulling the bird's head under water drowning it. The ingenuity of a good bushman was limitless, but Joe's diet during this period was probably augmented by friends who would leave an occasional cache of flour or some other commodity at a prearranged spot. The police had lost all interest in Joe's case and were quite prepared to believe that he had succeeded in crossing the border into South Australia, but eventually, almost exactly a year after his escape he was sighted.

On 5 March 1868 Constable Lally, stationed on the Victoria Plains, received word that Joe was hutkeeping at the far limits of the district. He set out for the place immediately, but on the 11th his horse, saddled and still wearing its bridle, returned to the station. Worried settlers sent word to Sergeant Kelly at Newcastle who with Constable Hayden, fearing that something was wrong, rushed to investigate. On arrival at the Victoria Plains police station they were informed that Lally was all right. Tracking Joe from the Moore River to Bindoon, he had made camp on the night of the 10th and had awoken to discover that his horse had broken its hobbles and headed for home. A long and weary walk to the police station then ensued before he was again mounted and back on the tracks. Kelly, hoping for Hayden's hat trick, sent that officer to join Lally with a native from the New Norcia Mission. The native returned to the mission on the 18th, stating that they had been following the tracks in a valley between Bindoon and Gingin when Joe had spotted them from a hill. The fugitive had taken to his heels and so cleverly covered his tracks that further pursuit was abandoned. Hayden had gone into Gingin to see if there was any news of Joe there and, if one recalls his past record where Joe was concerned, it is certain that he did not give up the chase easily.

'It appears', reported Kelly, 'that Johns has been between the beach and Bindoon and the Moore all the time and is in a most miserable plight with scarcely any clothes on him and so thin that you could nearly see through him.'[22]

In spite of Joe's plight and the ease with which tracks could be followed on sand-plain country, Joe was not sighted again and the

police made no further effort to run him down. There can be little
doubt that, while Joe was leading such a blameless life in the bush,
the police considered it a waste of money and manpower to continue
the hunt. However, more sinister reasons were adduced in a contemporary article, advancing the cruelty to convicts during Hampton's
administration. Referring to Joe, the article stated:

> How he escaped is a matter of surprise but why he was not followed
> but allowed to remain unmolested is still more extra-ordinary — What
> has become of him? It is a common question, and a very general
> impression prevails, that the revelations he could make would prove
> damaging to parties in high position.[23]

Not long after this Governor Hampton resigned and left Western
Australia, and until the arrival of Governor Weld the affairs of the
colony were administered by the commandant, Lieutenant-Colonel
Bruce. During Hampton's term dissatisfaction amongst the convicts
had been general and the appointment of his son to the post of acting
comptroller-general had done nothing to improve matters. Accusa-
tions of tyranny and oppression had been levelled against the latter
and it is evident that under his administration escape attempts had
become more numerous. Between June 1866 and March 1867 no less
than ninety convicts had attempted escape, three times the number
of any former similar period.[24] In spite of this, George Hampton
voiced his willingness to remain in the colony after his father had left,
provided the secretary of state appointed him officially as comptroller-
general. Using all the sarcasm it could muster, the local press reported this statement under the heading 'Good News'. The following
week the appointment of Henry Wakeford to the position was glee-
fully announced in the newspapers, and Hampton found himself out
of work. Wakeford, formerly police magistrate at Perth, took over in
May 1867, and in spite of the reaction to Joe's success the numbers
of escape attempts began to decrease almost immediately and had
all but ceased within two years, although one notable escape did
take place in 1869.

On 18 February 1869 John Boyle O'Reilly, an Irish political
prisoner, escaped and went into hiding. He later got clean away
from the colony aboard the American whaling ship *Gazelle*. O'Reilly
was a member of the revolutionary Fenian movement and had been

convicted for withholding evidence of an intended mutiny in the
10th Regiment. The death sentence was eventually commuted to
twenty years' transportation and he arrived in Western Australia in
January 1868 aboard the *Hougomont*, the last convict ship to arrive
in Australia. His good behaviour earned him a position of trust,
which together with the help of sympathetic locals made his escape
possible.[25] The year he spent in Western Australia made a deep
impression on him, and in later years this man would contribute
more than a little to the legend of Moondyne Joe.

REFERENCES

1. *Inquirer* 13 March 1867.
2. Police Records, WAA Acc. No. 129 10/463; *Perth Gazette* 22 March
   1867.
3. *Perth Gazette* 7 June 1867.
4. Convict Records, WAA Acc. No. 1156 R26.
5. C. Treadgold, 'Bushrangers in Western Australia', *Early Days,* vol. 2,
   October 1939, p. 49.
6. Convict Records, WAA Acc. No. 1156 R13.
7. Ibid R&D5.
8. *Perth Gazette* 7 June 1867.
9. Ibid.
10. Ibid.
11. Ibid 28 June, 5 July 1867.
12. Ibid 7 June 1867.
13. Ibid 14 June 1867.
14. Convict Records, WAA Acc. No. 1156 R&D5.
15. *Perth Gazette* 16, 23 August 1867.
16. Ibid 11 October 1867.
17. Ibid 23 August 1867.
18. Ibid 11 October 1867.
19. Ibid 30 August 1867.
20. Ibid 27 September 1867.
21. Ibid 6, 13, 27 September 1867.
22. Police Records, WAA Acc. No. 129 11/732.
23. *Fremantle Herald* 10 October 1868.
24. *Perth Gazette* 15 March 1867.
25. Douglas Pike, *Australian Dictionary of Biography,* vol. 5 (Melbourne:
    Melbourne University Press 1974), p. 371.

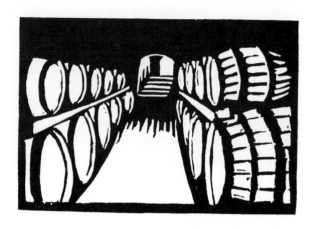

Chapter eleven

1869-1873

It was not until almost two years after his escape that Joe's life of freedom came to an end. The story of his capture can be told no better than by one who took part, Mr C. W. Ferguson of the Houghton Vineyard at Upper Swan. His memories of the affair are as follows:

> On February 25, 1869, when I was living at Upper Swan, I had been to Perth on business, and just after returning home I received a message stating that a man had been drowned in the river and requesting me to notify the police at Guildford. I did so, and two mounted troopers were despatched to undertake the dragging of the river at the spot where it was believed the man had been drowned. The troopers were assisted by about a dozen other men but it was not until about 1 o'clock the next morning that the body was recovered and taken by the police to the man's home. I had been one of the searchers, and invited the police officers and the others to come across to the cellars at the Houghton Vineyards, which I owned, and have a drink of wine, and we were all very wet and cold.
>
> Unknown to us at the time, another man, Moondyne Joe, had

17 Charles W. Ferguson, owner of Houghton Vineyard, where Joe was captured

18 The Houghton Vineyard cellar in which Joe was caught on 26 February
1869

selected that very night to force an entry to my wine cellars. He had
apparently come from far away in the hills. I knew Moondyne, whose
proper name was John Bolleto Johns [*sic*], fairly well. He was a tall
man, standing well over 6 ft in height, and although spare of build,
was extremely powerful and was a first rate bushman and rider. He
knew every inch of the country between the Helena River, the head of
the Swan, and Chittering Brook. He allowed his hair to grow in long
plaits over his shoulders, and he also grew a very long beard.[1]

Ferguson's acquaintance with Joe went back to Joe's horse-trapping
days when Ferguson's father had lost a pony and offered a £3
reward for its recovery. Joe found the pony, returned it to Houghton
and received the reward. The Fergusons asked him to put the animal
in a certain paddock, which he did, but next day the fence was found
to be cut and tracks showed that the horse had been driven out
through the gap. It was never seen again, and Joe was strongly
suspected of having a hand in its disappearance.

Ferguson continues:

In anticipation of the plunder he expected to carry away with him
from the cellars, he had cut a hole in the centre of a wheat sack and
fitted it over his head. In each end of the sack he had a two gallon
keg, one in front and one at the back. He had covered his boots with
sheep skins to disguise his tracks. In a small canvas bag around his
neck were six skeleton keys, a brass tap, a dark lantern, and a waddy
made from a piece of York gum, about 2 ft long.

It was unfortunate for Moondyne that he arrived at the cellars not
long before the police search party, at my invitation, also arrived.
When I put my key into the lock of the cellar door I found the door
unlocked, and it creaked ajar. I thought it was strange, but concluded
that it had not been closed when work had ceased for the day. I
therefore lighted a candle I was carrying and commenced to walk
along the cellar between the rows of wine barrels. The cellar was
about 60 ft long and the spluttering flame of the candle did little
more than light the few feet of space immediately in front of me.

One of my men was carrying a large jug, and we commenced to
walk towards a cask of wine which was on tap. We had only gone a
few yards from the door when there was an unearthly yell and the
tall figure of a man, with hair streaming over his shoulders and looking extremely weird, with the contrivance he carried over his head
and shoulders, sprang out of the darkness. He made a tremendous

blow at me with his waddy, which just grazed my shoulder, made a second plunge at the man who was carrying the jar, and dashed past us towards the door straight into the arms of the police officers and the other men who were following. The cellar had been plunged into darkness, as the candle had dropped from my hand, and my man had also dropped his jug. I confess that I was scared for the moment as, I think, most men would have been in similar circumstances, and was relieved when I got outside to find that my attacker had been captured by the police, and was sitting on the ground securely hand-cuffed. No one at first recognised the intruder, and then someone called out, "Why, its Moondyne."

"Yes", replied the prisoner, "you have got me at last."

Moondyne coolly asked me to give him a drink as he had not had time to get one for himself. He had, he declared, just put the tap he had brought with him into the cask when he heard voices outside, and was afraid that his arrival had been noticed, and that he would have to fight his way out. He said he was sorry he had struck me as he had no ill-will towards me. He also said he had seen my mother walking up and down whilst he had been hiding amongst the vines waiting an opportunity to break into the cellar. Moondyne had apparently lost control of himself somewhat, for, if he had only rolled under the numerous rows of gantrees in the cellar, I would have walked to the cask, filled the jug, and walked out again, and he would have been left undiscovered to make his way out at his leisure, after we had retired. Moondyne had arrived on horseback, and he asked me to allow someone to go and release his horse, which he had tied up at a place near by, known as the Sand Pit. I did so, but no horse was there, and it was evident that the animal had been released by one of his numerous friends.

It was Ferguson's belief that Joe intended stealing the wine to celebrate the second anniversary of his escape which was only eleven days off, but as it turned out, poor Joe was forced to celebrate in prison. He was escorted from Ferguson's by Sergeant Peacock and Constable McKay and delivered to Fremantle Prison by Constable King just after midnight, some twenty-four hours after his capture.[2] An article reporting the capture stated: 'Joe has informed the police that it is not his intention to stay long in this time.'[3] Prison officials were well aware of Joe's intentions and instructions were issued that his cell be inspected every thirty minutes day and night. The prisoner's meat was cut up for him and the only eating utensil allowed him was a wooden spoon with which to eat his soup. Even this had to be returned after each meal.[4]

A few days after his capture Joe was brought before the visiting magistrate and charged with absconding. He was sentenced to twelve months' additional imprisonment in irons, six months of which were to be passed in strict separate confinement.[5] On March 22 he was again brought before the visiting magistrate, this time for breaking and entering the premises of Mr Ferguson. For this latter charge he received a sentence of three years in irons.[6] An examination of Joe's record at this time (1869) shows that he was not now due for release until 1884 when he would be in his late fifties. Incarcerated as he was in his special cell,[7] his situation appeared hopeless, but whatever can be said about Joe, he was never a quitter.

In September he wrote to the comptroller-general, making a full statement of all the circumstances of his case and again protesting his innocence of the original charge laid against him.[8] This, coupled with his good behaviour, did have some effect. About four months later a remission of five years' gang labour was approved.[9] Naturally enough this could hardly satisfy a man who considered himself innocent. Unfortunately Joe's letters have not survived, but the granting of the remission helps prove the strength of his arguments.

During this period repeated claims for a reward for Joe's capture were made by John Mann and James West. Although the details are lost, it is assumed that these two were present at Ferguson's cellars and were directly responsible for checking Joe's headlong rush for freedom. Whatever the real circumstances all their claims were refused, though the official reaction may have been different if Hampton had still been governor.

A little over a year after his capture, Joe begged to be released from irons but his request was completely ignored. No evidence remains to show how Joe was standing up to the long hours of confinement in his tiny cell but there were no complaints about his behaviour. On 10 September 1870 he was loaned a pair of spectacles,[10] and just five days later, Comptroller-General Wakeford asked the superintendent to report on the expediency of releasing prisoner number 8189 from irons.[11] Lefroy was of the opinion that Joe's good behaviour had earned him release from the irons and suggested that the prisoner be employed in the carpenter's shop. For security reasons he was not to be allowed outside the gate of the mechanic's yard. Wakeford saw fit to recommend this suggestion, and nineteen months after they had been fitted, the iron manacles were struck off. Once again Joe had the use of his hands.

His first act was to write to Wakeford and enquire when his sentence would expire.[12] This letter also appears to have been completely ignored, in view of which, after waiting three months for a reply, Joe decided on a more positive course of action. On 21 February 1871 he was found to be varying his work in the carpenter's shop by surreptitiously filing a key for his cell. Upon being discovered he managed to hurl both key and file over the prison wall. What became of them after that was never clear, but Joe's quick thinking certainly saved him from receiving a further additional sentence. In the absence of both key and file the visiting magistrate had no option but to dismiss the charge of attempted escape brought against him. At this time Joe was also mixed up with a fellow-prisoner named Ingram. The pair appear to have been writing 'clandestine letters'; unfortunately, no details have survived apart from the fact that Joe managed to avoid the punishment meted out to Ingram. Such behaviour however could not be overlooked completely and Joe was banned from the carpenter's shop and again put to work breaking stones within the prison walls. This time his stone heap was placed away from the wall near the stringent-discipline class.

In April Wakeford spoke with Joe about his situation and elicited a scrap of information that was to make all the difference. Joe recalled Governor Hampton promising him his freedom if he could escape again and Wakeford immediately contacted Lefroy to check if Hampton's remark could be verified. Lefroy replied that the exact words spoken were: 'If you get out again I'll forgive you.' On being informed of his predecessor's promise, Governor Weld agreed that, under the circumstances, additional punishment seemed unfair. Wakeford spent some time investigating Joe's case and finally it was decided to release the latter on a ticket of leave to the Vasse depot. If he stayed out of trouble for four years, he was told, he could expect a conditional pardon.

On discharge from Fremantle Joe was supplied with a complete new rig-out including boots, socks, tweed trousers, three shirts, a jacket, cap and two handkerchiefs.[13] Still bemused by his sudden change of luck, Joe sailed for Busselton on May 13.[14] Busselton on the Vasse River lay on the coast about 200 kilometres south of Fremantle and was considered far enough away from Joe's old haunts to allay any further escape attempts. The town boasted three hotels and was the main port for the Vasse district.

It was two months before it dawned on Joe that a reduced sentence was hardly sufficient for an innocent man. As soon as he realized this, he dashed off a letter to Wakeford demanding a certificate of freedom. The comptroller-general instructed Joseph Harris, the resident magistrate at Busselton to inform Joe that only an unblemished record until July 1875 would procure him such a certificate. Joe promptly applied for a pass to Perth to obtain legal advice on his case, but Harris referred his request to Wakeford who firmly refused and stated that Joe should be satisfied.

At this time Joe was employed by Henry Yelverton, one of the first timber contractors to recognize the worth of convict labour.[15] He probably worked at Yelverton's sawmill at Quindalup, about 19 kilometres west of Busselton. The correspondence regarding Joe's pass was forwarded to Yelverton's office and in his absence was appropriated by Joe.[16] Presumably Joe intended to turn it over to his prospective solicitor but he was finally persuaded to return it by Harris.

Denied the opportunity of aquiring legal aid in Perth Joe now petitioned the governor. In the face of this constant badgering, Governor Weld and Comptroller-General Wakeford finally agreed to another remission of twelve months, with the prospect of further remission providing Joe's good conduct continued. Advice of this decision was sent to W. P. Clifton, the resident magistrate at Bunbury, with a note requesting him to inform Joe who had apparently moved there from Busselton in the interim, Bunbury being about 48 kilometres closer to Perth. Seeing little hope of further concessions, Joe settled down and stayed out of trouble. Obtaining work as a shepherd for a Donnybrook settler named Yarackie Woods, he camped at Queenwood on the Preston River for a time. It was at this camp that E. H. Withers first made Joe's acquaintance. Out possum hunting one night, young Withers became lost. After stumbling around in the dark for a while he at last heard the tinkling of sheep bells which led him directly to Joe's campfire. Many years later Withers recalled the friendly welcome he received from the bushman. Joe showed him how to skin and tan the pelts of the few possums he had shot, gave him a bed for the remainder of the night and next day accompanied him back to his own camp.[17] Shepherding was only seasonal work so Joe eventually returned to Bunbury, where before long he found himself behind bars once again.

Although complete details are not available, it appears that Joe had ventured into an erotic and somewhat shady new enterprise. In August 1872 the Bunbury police found him in possession of cantharides (Spanish fly), strychnine and a liquid of his own concoction which was said to procure abortions. Forseeing the loss of his ticket of leave, Joe lost control and assaulted Constable Hay. He apparently also behaved badly in the lockup because Clifton, reporting the affair to Wakeford, cast doubts on Joe's sanity.

Within days the law took its course and Joe was sentenced to one month's imprisonment. For health reasons and to make life on the run difficult for would-be absconders, all inmates of Fremantle Prison had to have their hair and beards removed. Joe apparently kicked up such a fuss about this that Clifton was moved to suggest that the rules be relaxed in his case. Wakeford was inclined to agree and ordered both the superintendent and the surgeon to leave Joe's hair alone when he arrived from Bunbury, but to keep him under strict surveillance regarding his sanity. But Joe, with hair intact, was calm and well-behaved. Towards the end of his sentence he asked Wakeford to allow him to serve the remainder of his ticket-of-leave time in Fremantle. Wakeford agreed, and after completing his month in the prison, Joe was discharged to the Fremantle depot.[18]

He found work as a carpenter with Robert Wrightson, a well known boat-builder, and apparently became interested in the work. His behaviour was exemplary and, within nine months, Wakeford recommended that he be issued a certificate of freedom. This was approved by the governor,[19] and Joe finally became a free man again on 27 June 1873.[20]

Almost eight years had passed since Joe had received his ten years' sentence. During that time he had spent less than four years behind bars. He had escaped repeatedly, outwitting both prison authorities and the police. His determination not to serve the sentence does much to show that Joe sincerely believed in his own innocence. The consideration and kindness shown him by Cowan, Lefroy, Wakeford and Governor Weld shows that at least some doubts as to his guilt existed in the minds of officialdom. The general public, especially those of convict background, regarded Joe's escapades with tolerance, and there was a certain amount of respect for one who had so often dared to defy authority. His exploits were recounted with relish wherever men met and yarned. The legend had begun.

REFERENCES

1. *Sunday Times* 27 May 1928.
2. Convict Records, WAA Acc. No. 1156 C32-595; Police Records, WAA Acc. No. 129 12/922, 12/958.
3. *Fremantle Herald* 27 February 1869.
4. Convict Records, WAA Acc No. 1156 S012-31, 36.
5. Convict Records, WAA Acc. No. 1156 C50-7464; Police Records, WAA Acc. No. 129 12/922.
6. *Fremantle Herald* 27 March 1869.
7. Convict Records, WAA Acc. No. 1156 S012-47.
8. Ibid C49-6087.
9. Ibid C50-7464.
10. Ibid V14.
11. Ibid C50-7464.
12. Ibid C52-12759.
13. Ibid V23A.
14. Ibid C52-12759.
15. Rodger Jennings, The Story of Henry Yelverton of Quindalup, WAA PR767.
16. Convict Records, WAA Acc. No. 1156 C52-12759.
17. Memories of E. H. Withers, WAA HS/574.
18. Ibid SO12-93.
19. Ibid C52-12759.
20. Ibid R21B.

Chapter twelve

Life was comparatively quiet in Fremantle in the 1870s. Under the fair administration of Weld and Wakeford convict unrest became a thing of the past and escape attempts were rare. Only one escape worthy of notice occurred during this period. On Easter Monday, 17 April 1876 a furious tolling of the prison alarm-bell signalled the disappearance of six Irish political prisoners from their places of employment.

The absconders were Fenians and friends of John Boyle O'Reilly (see Chapter Ten) and the escape had been organized by American agents of the Clan-na-Gael Society. John Breslin, who had previously organized the escape of another Fenian from a prison in Dublin, was responsible for getting the prisoners away from Fremantle to a whaleboat waiting on the beach near Rockingham. The boat was from the American whaling ship *Catalpa* commanded by Captain George Anthony. The ship was owned by the Clan-na-Gael Society and her presence was no accident. The rescue was well planned and went without a hitch. Even as the alarm-bell clanged, Breslin and

119

the absconders were being rowed across Cockburn Sound towards
the *Catalpa*, standing off and on some 24 kilometres beyond Garden
Island.

The steamer *Georgette* was commandeered by the water police to
approach the *Catalpa*, but although she reached the whaler early
the next morning before the escapees, lack of coal forced her to
return to Fremantle almost immediately. Despite a lookout at the
masthead, the police aboard the steamer did not sight the whaleboat which kept on its course towards the *Catalpa*, where the Fenians
were able to clamber aboard only minutes before the arrival of a
water-police cutter. The ten-man detail in the cutter were powerless
to prevent the whaling ship from sailing and were soon left far
behind.

Back at Fremantle, a large crowd had gathered to await the
return of the *Georgette*. No doubt Joe was in their midst and firmly
on the side of the absconders. The news that the escape had been
successful was received happily by most, but the drama was far
from over. The *Georgette* was refueled and a twelve-pound field-gun
was mounted on her decks. She set out in pursuit of the *Catalpa*
late that night and caught up with her during the following morning.
A shot was fired across the whaleship's bow to halt the American
vessel, but Captain Anthony pointed to his flag and sailed on. The
affair fizzled out in an anticlimax. Unwilling to risk international
repercussions, those aboard the *Georgette* could do nothing but
return to Fremantle, leaving the rejoicing Irishmen to continue
their voyage to America and a life of freedom.

It was probably around the time of their triumphant arrival in
America that John Boyle O'Reilly began work on a novel dealing
with convictism in Western Australia. The novel was called *Moondyne* and the central character was none other than 'Moondyne
Joe', but the exploits of the dashing hero bear little resemblance to
those of Joseph Johns. Nevertheless the book did much to promote
the ever-growing legends and tales about our Joe.

O'Reilly's Joe is transported for poaching deer to feed his poor
starving mother and sisters. His convict number is 406, a number of
strange significance to O'Reilly.[1] Convict records show that 406 was
really a man named William Whittle.[2] After O'Reilly's Joe arrives
in Western Australia, he is bonded to a villainous devil named

Bowman who works him as a slave. Joe is finally goaded into attacking his master and is forced to flee into the bush. There he is befriended by the 'Vasse' tribe who come to revere him. They call him 'Moondyne', meaning, according to O'Reilly, something 'more than either manhood or kingship'. When he is recaptured the natives assist him to escape and disclose to him the whereabouts of their secret gold mine, a huge cavern in the hills near Busselton. After an adventure with his ex-master, now turned policeman, which ends in the latter's death in an inland desert, Joe uses the native's vast store of gold to finance him in returning to England. Under the name of Mr Wyeville and armed with a special commission from the Queen, he brings about tremendous prison reforms and returns to the penal colony of Western Australia in the position of comptroller-general. His reforms are applied with outstanding success but Joe, gallant and noble to the end, finally perishes in a bushfire in a vain attempt to save two travellers.

There can be no doubt that the real Joe's exploits laid the foundation for O'Reilly's fantasy, and in some ways the book was to prove strangely prophetic. But when it was published in 1879 Joe had several years of comparative respectability behind him.

According to Memories of E. H. Withers, Joe in 1875 worked for a time in a sawmill at Lockville near Busselton. Joe, E. H. Withers and a man named George Woods worked together on one of the saws there, but by July 1876 Joe was again residing at Fremantle.

There was one small lapse in May 1877 when he appeared in the Fremantle Police Court charged with 'unlawful possession of an iron knee'. Apparently he was again in the boat-building business, 'knee' being the nautical term for brackets holding the thwarts of a boat rigidly to the sides and gunwales. Being unable to explain satisfactorily how the object came into his possession, he was fined £5 with a threat of three months' imprisonment in default.[3] Presumably he paid the fine.

February 1878 found him enlisting the aid of the police in recovering some stolen property.[4] It appears that, when Joe had left Fremantle on a journey through the hills in July 1876, a box containing some of his belonging had been left in the care of an acquaintance of his known as 'Walker, alias Wilson, alias Osborne's baker'. Amongst other items the box contained Joe's watch and a gold chain with a sovereign attached. Walker took to wearing these around Fremantle for a time and then transferred them to another man said to be his 'uncle'. Walker himself moved to Northampton, but Joe's complaint caused him to be brought back to stand trial at the Supreme Court criminal sittings to be held on Wednesday 3 April 1878. Walker's case did not go before the court at that time,[5] and it is presumed that Joe's property had been returned and the case dropped.

In 1879 Joe was listed in the Postal Directory of the day as a 'boatbuilder'.[6] Whether he had his own business at this time or was again working for Wrightson is not known. He appears to have been something of a dandy during this period of his life. The gold watch chain, commonly referred to as an 'albert' after Prince Albert who had made them fashionable, was generally worn in the waistcoat of a three-piece suit, which indicates a considerable improvement in Joe's standard of dress. He had met a young widow, Louisa Hearn (*née* Braddick), and he and Louisa were married in the Johnston Memorial Congregational Church at Fremantle on 16 January 1879.[7] The witnesses were C. Henry Gwynne and Caroline Reynolds. Joe was then in his early fifties; Louisa was only twenty-six.

June 1880 found Louisa and Joe in the Vasse district and a fascinating conjecture arises. Had Joe read O'Reilly's novel? Did he dream of finding a secret store of gold at the Vasse? Alas, we shall never know for sure.

He and Louisa, in the company of their friend, George Woods, hiked south from Busselton.[8] They asked for work at 'Ellensbrook', the property of John Brockman, but Mrs Brockman advised them to go on to her father's place. Mrs Frances Brockman was the daughter of Alfred Bussell, the owner of 'Wallcliffe' near the mouth of the Margaret River. On their arrival at Wallcliffe both men were hired, Joe at £3 and Woods at £2 per month. Presumably Joe received the extra in consideration of Louisa's helping out in the kitchen. John Brockman was apparently away at this time and his wife paid frequent visits to Wallcliffe. It is her pen that delightfully describes the daily happenings in that historic old homestead and at her own place Ellensbrook, during this period.

Joe worked on both properties and his woodworking prowess was in great demand. His first job was hanging a gate down by the river, after which he and Woods were busily occupied for some days in splitting palings and erecting a substantial fence around the garden. They proved their usefulness as handymen when they repaired the mangle, and in late July they were given the task of repairing all the fences around Bussell's Cowaramup paddocks.

Both men appear to have been satisfactory workers, and although Joe made a few mistakes, they were regarded as honest ones. Once he carelessly let two horses out and a full day was wasted in tracking and returning them to their paddock. An entry in Mrs Brockman's diary for August 4 reads: 'Joe (Moondyne) and Woods killed beef and oh what a terrible bother we had. Joe missed our own bullock we picked out for killing and killed a strange bullock belonging to Guerin.' One can imagine the tongue-lashing he would have received for his poor aim. Frances Brockman was not one to hide her feelings as an incident concerning her Chinese cook shows: 'I had a great to do with my chinaman this morning. I gave him some steak to grill and he burnt it to a chip and I expostulated with him somewhat warmly and he threw a pot of rice at my feet and I gave him a little wholesome connection with the broomhandle.' A few days later there was more trouble with the fellow: 'Joe came over for me. The horrid chinaman is going to summons Papa so he went to town. Mrs. Johns went in too for a witness against the chinaman.'

Joe continued working for Bussell, ploughing, chaff-cutting and doing odd jobs although Louisa ceased her chores in the kitchen. 'Mrs. Johns and old Coe had a fight,' wrote Mrs Brockman in December. 'She has left the kitchen. Now I do my own cooking again.'

In January 1881 Joe and George Woods were sent to do a month's work at Mr Maurice Davies's timber mill. Davies was one of the first to export karri timber and his mill at Karridale, situated about 32 kilometres south of the Margaret River, was the centre of a thriving settlement at that time. The sawn timber was shipped from nearby Hamelin Bay. Life at the timber mill apparently agreed with Joe and he decided to stay on there. In March, Mrs Brockman noted: 'Joe Johns and Mrs. Johns have gone for good.'

One of Joe's workmates at Karridale was a young man named Gavin McGregor with whom he became friendly. They worked side by side for several years and McGregor's memories of him are worth repeating. Asked to comment when in his seventy-sixth year, McGregor stated that Joe was a tireless and honest worker, the kind of man he would have unhesitatingly chosen to accompany him on any mission. Tall, straight and wiry, he had a pleasing countenance and was deservedly popular with his workmates. He never boasted, and when the subject of his escapes came up, he repeatedly swore his innocence. To charges of bushranging he replied that he only stole from the settlers when circumstances forced him to. According to McGregor, Joe's only weakness was 'language'. In an exasperating situation 'he could cause the most proficient bullocky to sit up and take notice.'[9]

Joe must have spat out a blistering stream of this 'language' during an incident that occurred in September 1881. He interfered in some way with a local resident's dog and the animal leapt upon him and bit part of his ear off. A correspondent from the Vasse district informed a city newspaper that 'Joe intends to claim damages from the owner of the dog for the loss he has sustained'.[10] Nevertheless later developments are unknown.

19 Main chamber of Moondyne Cave

During their spare time at Karridale Joe and McGregor explored the surrounding country on horseback. During one of these jaunts Joe discovered the cave that now bears his name. It was not filled with gold like the cave in O'Reilly's novel, but it did contain some spectacular formation and proved a popular tourist attraction for many years during the next century.

In 1883 Joe moved to Bunbury and obtained work with a well-known contractor named Floyd. Joe, E. H. Withers and a man named Jim White spent six weeks together camped on the Ferguson River constructing a bridge. After that Joe and Withers worked in Floyd's workshop for about two years. Withers recalls that George Woods resided with Joe and Louisa during this period.[11]

Exactly when Joe left Bunbury is uncertain, however the year 1887 found him back at Newcastle and in no time he was in trouble again.[12] He fell into debt to Arthur Wroth, Newcastle's butcher, and there seemed to be no way of repaying the money. In June that year Wroth entered into a contract with Millar Bros who held large timber leases on the south side of the York road along Helena Brook.[13] There were good stands of jarrah there and the recently completed 'Eastern Railway' had made the area accessible to timber merchants. A sawmill run by Sexton Bros was situated on Chauncy Gully within Millar Bros leases, and Wroth apparently agreed to cart the sawn timber from there to the nearest railway station 'Chidlows Well'. Joe asked to be allowed to work off his liability on this job, to which Wroth agreed.

The terms of the agreement were simple. Joe was to have the use of one of Wroth's drays and two horses. He would receive the benefit of such work as he performed except for ten per cent which was to be paid to Wroth by way of rent for the team. Wroth hoped that Joe would soon make enough money to repay his debt.

'Chidlows Well' (now called Chidlow) was then an important stopping place on the old railway line. The place has a history of refreshing thirsty travellers. The original well was a popular watering-place for wayfarers on the old Northam road in the early days, and after the construction of the railway it was there that the water tanks of the steam locomotives were refilled. Joe no doubt sought refreshment at the 'Oxford Inn', a rambling weatherboard establishment situated on the south side of the line and run by John

20 The old Perth lockup

Symonds.[14] It is likely too that both he and Louisa resided at 'Chidlows Well' during this period, probably in a rough bush hut with the iron roof and hessian walls so typical of the times.

In early November Joe sent word for Wroth to come and collect his team. According to Wroth an arrangement was made whereby Joe was to cart a shed to Newcastle and deliver the dray and horses there, but Joe never arrived. Wroth set out to look for him and eventually located him in Perth at Johnson's boarding-house in Murray Street. When he asked after his team, Joe said he could see it but that was all. On arriving at the stables at the rear of the boarding-house, Joe allegedly threatened Wroth with an axe and told him he would chop him down if he took the team away. Wroth hurriedly withdrew and rushed around to the police station, where Detective Connor was detailed to investigate the matter.

Connor proceeded immediately to the boarding-house, but Joe hotly denied everything and maintained that he was buying the dray, horses and three sets of harness and had twelve months to pay for them. He had no bill of sale, so the horses were taken to the police stables. Joe was arrested and thrown into the Perth lockup to await trial on a charge of theft. He was then aged about sixty and the years had taken their toll. He made no attempt to escape.

REFERENCES

1. James Jeffrey Roche, *Life, Poems and Speeches of John Boyle O'Reilly* (New York: Cassell Publishing Co 1891).
2. Convict Records, WAA Acc. No. 1156 R1B.
3. *Inquirer* 16 May 1877.
4. *Herald* 9 February 1878.
5. Ibid 6 April 1878.
6. *The Western Australian Almanac and Directory for 1879* (Perth: Stirling Bros 1879), p. xi.
7. Mary Tamblyn, Research in 1968, WAA 2086A.
8. Diary of Frances Brockman, WAA 938A.
9. *South Western News* 8 April 1932.
10. *Herald* 1 October 1881.
11. Memories of E. H. Withers. WAA HS/574.
12. *West Australian* 18 November 1887.
13. Original Plan Swan 131, Lands and Surveys Department.
14. Original Plan Resumptions 347, Lands and Surveys Department.

Chapter thirteen

1887-1900

By a strange coincidence, while Joe was cooling his heels in the Perth lockup, a spate of jail breaks occurred at Fremantle Prison. The first of these took place on the morning of Tuesday 15 November 1887.[1] The escapee, a man named William Thompson, was said to have had no equal as a prison breaker excepting perhaps Moondyne Joe himself. But Thompson had not gained a reputation for peaceable behaviour as had Joe.

In 1880 Thompson had absconded from a work party in Government Gardens and begun a reign of terror in the York and Beverley districts. At the latter place he had broken into a cottage where he tortured and raped the housewife who resided there. He had been captured after a gun battle with the police and sentenced to death, but the governor and Executive Council had taken a merciful view of his case and commuted his sentence to life imprisonment. Some time later he had escaped again and committed several robberies around Pinjarra.[2] The police seemed unable to catch him, so a number of settlers had banded together and gone in pursuit. They

had come up with Thompson at night but he had refused to surrender. One of the McLartys had put a bullet through his shoulder
to stop him and it was reported that Thompson had sworn vengeance
on the McLartys. Understandably there was some uneasiness felt at
Pinjarra when he was reported to have once more made his escape.

The first report of the escape stated that it was made with outside
help, that a rope had been fastened to the outside of the wall,
thrown over the top and a pile of civilian clothing was stashed
nearby. This report was later contradicted when it was said that
Thompson had made his own rope from the material used for
sewing hammocks in the prison workshop. The rope was fastened to
the end of a trouser leg filled with sand and hurled over the wall by
Thompson himself. Whatever the real story, his absence was not
noticed for some time and he succeeded in getting clean away. Just
twenty-four hours later Thomas Hughes and James Jarvis made
their escape from Fremantle.[3]

Hughes was a desperate character who had been suspected of
several burglaries earlier in the year. The police had kept a close
watch on him, and on the evening of April 17 Constables Franklin
and O'Connell had met him near the outskirts of Fremantle. They
followed him and he began to run. As he tried to climb through a
fence, the police had grabbed his leg whereupon Hughes had turned
and fired a shot, killing Constable O'Connell. He then took to the
bush, and in spite of a massive police hunt, managed to remain
at large for nearly three months. Three times the police had him at
bay, but each time he had got away after an exchange of shots. He
was finally captured after a furious gun battle with the police in
July and only surrendered after being hit in the thigh. He received a
life sentence for manslaughter.

Jarvis was perhaps less of a desperado than Hughes and did not
have his partner's intimate knowledge of the bush. He was a sailor
and had stolen a boat from Augusta. A passing ship had picked
him up off Hamelin Bay and he was subsequently conveyed to
prison. He broke prison but was recaptured and sentenced to
cumulative sentences amounting to eight months. At the time of his
escape with Hughes, Jarvis had only five weeks of his sentence left to
serve.

The escape was executed with the cool daring typical of Hughes's past exploits. He and Jarvis were with a group of prisoners working within the prison walls. An excavation for a tank was being dug near the prison hospital and the men were directed by an unarmed warder. About 15 metres away stood a sentry armed with a double-barrelled gun. At about 9.30 am, Jarvis left the pit and walked to the toolshed which was beside the sentry's beat. Hughes also left the pit and went to the tap. The sentry Alexander Rogers kept a close watch on Hughes, but while his back was turned, Jarvis came out of the toolshed and grabbed him from behind.[4] Hughes stepped up, knocked Rogers down and took the gun. Thus armed, he and Jarvis ordered both warders into a nearby toilet and locked them in. Hughes then turned the gun on the bemused prisoners and ordered them to lean a long plank against the wall. Jarvis then climbed up and dropped over the top. When Hughes began to scale the plank, a prisoner named Green attempted to pull it away from the wall but Hughes fired at him, and although he missed, this gave him a few precious seconds to reach the top of the wall and disappear over the top. The whole affair had taken only a few minutes and was thought to have been carefully planned in advance.

As soon as news of the escape spread a police party rushed to the scene and were able to follow the escapees' tracks over 'Monument Hill' and towards North Lake. Although by the following day some forty police were in the field, their efforts were in vain. A Mrs Davies came across Hughes in the act of reloading his gun, but he assured her that he meant her no harm and went on his way.[5] Shortly afterward he passed some workmen and sang out gaily to them that he did not intend doing time for 'old Leake'. (George Walpole Leake was then acting chief justice and had pronounced sentence on Hughes.) A little further on Hughes met an old lady on the road. He told her that he was beginning a long journey and asked for a loaf of bread. This was supplied and he again went on his way.

Hughes had acted in a reasonable manner during all of these encounters but the authorities did not expect this to last. In fact it was thought that he and Jarvis might team up with Thompson and there was much apprehension on this account, so much so that a special notice was inserted in the *Government Gazette* on November 17, offering £200 reward for both Thompson and Hughes or £100 for either of them. Full descriptions of them were given and legal advice to persons other than the police who wished to attempt their capture was also included. Whether any private citizens did shoulder arms and join in the chase is not known, but the police search that followed was certainly one of the most intensive ever organized. A report in the *West Australian* reads:

> Orders were given by the Commissioner of Police (Captain Phillips) which had the effect of breaking up the police into parties stretching from Moore's paddock on the south bank of the river to the north bank. Inspector Lodge and party, travelling at a great pace, covered the country as far as the Jarrahdale Arms, visiting the houses of all the settlers and woodcutters on the way, and warning them of the escape of the three men. Sub-Inspector Lawrence worked the northern side of the river from the Limekilns round into Fremantle; P.C. Bonner and party took the northern bank of the river towards Bullen's Hotel; Corporal Hogan worked out in the direction of North Lake; and Sergeant Claffey came down through the Lower Canning into Moore's paddock. During the whole of Wednesday they pushed on inland through the bush and one of the parties, we believe, struck the right track at the Lower Canning. The police have with them the York native, who, during Hughes previous career of bushranging never made a single mistake in tracking. With the accuracy of a sleuth hound he followed the escapee's tracks on soft ground and even over ironstone, and was never at fault, though Hughes frequently changed his boots. It was upon his arrival on the scene of operations that the police began that hot chase of Hughes in which he was never given rest until he was run down on July 2, in Moore's paddock. By Wednesday evening Hughes and his partner must have obtained a good start; as at 11 a.m. he was seen at the Lower Canning by some men. Both he and Jarvis were barefooted, and Hughes was carrying the gun. These men did not know that any convicts had escaped. Hughes, however, said to an old man, at the Lower Canning, "They will have to put a bullet through Tom Hughes' heart before they will take him." At that time the two men were making towards the Lower Canning, near Mr. Nicolay's place. It was evident from the direction they were taking that they were on for the Darling Hills. The police parties camped in the bush on Wednesday night and were astir at daybreak. When once it was discovered that they had got again upon the tracks of the escapee's, the police parties closed in and joined. They then went along the tracks, Sub-Inspector Lawrence and party

leading the way, and during yesterday afternoon they were nearing the Darling Hills.[6]

The same report indicated that 'the police arrangements [seemed] to be of the most perfect character', but soon afterwards it became known that the runaways had given the police the slip and doubled back. When darkness fell on the Thursday night the tracks had been followed back to 'Cornish's place about five miles from Perth on the Albany road'.

Hughes and Jarvis reached Guildford during the following night and, desperate for supplies and clothing, Hughes broke into Padbury, Loton and Co's store there.[7] News of the robbery was telegraphed to Captain Phillips on Saturday morning and police reinforcements were sent to Guildford at once. Sergeant Claffey was scouring the bush in the Darling Range when he heard the news and he and his native assistant were the first to join the Guildford police in the search. But the tracks were totally confusing, going first one way and then another, so that no-one could tell which direction the escapees intended to take. While Claffey and the Guildford police were puzzling over the muddle of tracks at Guildford, Corporal Hackett and Constable O'Hara and their trackers, all well mounted and well armed, were beating up the north bank of the river from Perth. This party surprised the fugitives near Bassendean. Jarvis had a sprained ankle and was nearly blind with ophthalmia, and Hughes looked exhausted. They gave up without a fight, were duly handcuffed and escorted back to Perth.

Quite a crowd gathered at the Perth police station when they were brought in, and the commissioner himself went down to have a look at them. By his orders a horse-drawn Black Maria was sent for to convey the prisoners to the lockup, while mounted police had to be used to keep the milling crowd at bay. Reporting the excitement the *West Australian* (21 November 1887) stated:

> At about half past five, Hughes was brought out of the station heavily manacled, a constable also holding on to his handcuffs. As he came out of the doorway, there was a broad laugh upon his face and he smiled upon the crowd until placed in the van. Little attention was given to Jarvis, who also was placed in the van. A constable entered the van along with the prisoners and two others rode alongside it. As

the van was about to move away, a man in the crowd cried out,
"Three cheers for Tom Hughes", and a few people responded, but
there were more people who hooted than cheered. Then someone
called for cheers for the police and the response was hearty.

Hughes was tried at the Fremantle Police Court on the following
Friday and was sentenced to receive three dozen lashes with the
cat-o'-nine-tails for escaping and three years' hard labour in irons
for burglary.[8] During the trial he swore that Jarvis was innocent of
the burglary and shouldered the whole blame himself. It was
rumoured that he would never receive the lashes because he was
suffering from consumption,[9] but this later proved to be untrue.[10]
Jarvis got off with only three months' hard labour.[11]

During this time nothing had been heard of William Thompson.
Then on the Wednesday following Hughes's appearance in court,
he was captured at his camp near the Helena River by Corporal
Hogan and Constable Savage.[12] The camp was about 6 kilometres
from Smith's sawmill (now Glen Forrest) and Thompson had been
employed by a ticket-of-leave holder who was working on a fencing
contract. In return for a supply of food and 'protection' he had
agreed to bore post holes at night for his 'mate'. Apparently the
work was nearly completed when the 'mate' went to Subinspector
Lawrence and informed him of Thompson's whereabouts. The
police surprise was complete and Thompson surrendered without
resistance. He was sentenced to three years' hard labour in irons.

If his 'mate' expected to share in the reward he was sadly mistaken.
The money was shared three ways between Lawrence, Hogan and
Savage. Hackett and O'Hara were awarded £40 each for the capture
of Hughes and the remainder was shared between their trackers. So
ended what was probably one of the last bushranging incidents to
take place in Western Australia. The escapees were defeated by the
advent of telegraphic communications and the ability of an affluent
government to offer substantial rewards.

During all the excitement Joe and his solicitor, Mr Harvey, were
engaged in the legal wrangle with Wroth. While Hughes and Jarvis
were being tracked near North Lake, Joe's case was being heard at
the Perth Police Court.[13] Mr Harvey reserved his defence at that
time and the bench held that a *prima facie* case had been made
out. Joe was committed for trial by jury at the next criminal session

of the Supreme Court. He was granted bail at £100, but was allowed
to sign personally for only half that amount. No doubt the magistrates were influenced by his past record when they insisted on two
approved sureties of £25 each to make up the remainder. But Joe
was not without friends. The sureties were duly obtained and he
found himself once more a free man, at least until the Supreme
Court hearing was due.

There can be little doubt that he was one of the crowd at the
police station in Barrack Street when Hughes and Jarvis were brought
in, which makes one wonder about the identity of the fellow who
sung out, 'Three cheers for Tom Hughes.' At least we can be sure
that Joe was not among those who hooted and jeered.

On the following Friday the newspapers announced that the
attorney-general had declined to prosecute Joe in the Supreme
Court.[14] Apparently he considered the evidence against Joe too
flimsy, and as a result all charges were dropped. Joe was jubilant
and, within a week, he was reported to have commenced an action
against Wroth for false imprisonment, claiming £250 damages.[15]
There is no indication that this ever went to court, but three days
before Christmas, Wroth sued Joe for £90 for detaining the horses.[16]
That Joe was under the impression that the horses were his, although
still unpaid for, is shown by a report of his statement in court:

> Prior to obtaining the team I owed plaintiff £83. It was arranged
> that, provided I could pay him between £30 and £50 that week, I was
> to have a team for 12 months to work out the debt of £83 with
> interest at 10 per cent upon the value of the team. I paid him £38
> during the week off the £80 I was to pay for the team. I have no
> receipt for the £38 and it does not appear on my accounts. Wroth
> sold me the team for £80. There was to have been a written agree-
> ment but defendant neglected to draw it up.[17]

Under cross-examination he insisted that he did not have to complete payment for the team until June the following year. Two of
Joe's acquaintances, William Johnson and William Wing, swore
that they had heard Wroth refer to the team as 'your team' when in
conversation with Joe at the Royal Hotel. Wroth denied this emphatically, and in giving judgement the magistrate stated that he
saw no evidence of any sale having taken place. Wroth's claim was

not granted but Joe was instructed to return the team forthwith and there the affair rested. Joe's name disappeared from the newspaper columns and he appears to have stayed out of trouble for the next few years.

On several occasions he managed to slip the chains of domesticity and escape to the bush life he loved. On Tuesday 28 February 1888 Police Constable Lee of the Williams police station recorded as a traveller on the Albany road 'one Joseph Johns, alias "Moondyne Joe", from Perth to Williams, kangaroo hunting'.[18]

In May 1889 he again took his leave from Louisa and returned briefly to that place of promised wealth, the Vasse district. Perhaps O'Reilly's golden cave was only a dream; nevertheless there were other minerals that could make a man's fortune. Promising indications of graphite and coal had recently been discovered near Busselton, so it seems that Joe knew of country worth examining. Aboard the mailboat *Rob Roy* when she steamed out of Cockburn Sound that May, was a prospecting party consisting of Mr F. L. von Bibra and Mr L. S. Eliot, accompanied by their guide Mr Joseph B. Johns, 'better known as Moondyne Joe'.[19] The party disembarked at Busselton, hired a trap and horses and set out for the Margaret River. After about a week of stormy weather, they returned to Busselton and left for Fremantle by the next steamship. The whole enterprise appears to have been cloaked in secrecy. In the absence of any statement from the prospectors, Busselton was alive with various rumous for some time, but eventually the affair was forgotten and it must be assumed that the prospecting venture was a failure.[20]

REFERENCES

1. *Daily News* 15 November 1887.
2. *West Australian* 30 November 1887.
3. Ibid 17 November 1887.
4. Ibid 26 November 1887.
5. *Daily News* 17 November 1887.
6. *West Australian* 18 November 1887.
7. Ibid 21 November 1887.
8. Ibid 26, 28 November 1887.
9. *Daily News* 29 November 1887.
10. *West Australian* 1 December 1887.

11. Ibid 21 December 1887.
12. *West Australian* 2 December 1887; *Daily News* 17 December 1887.
13. *Daily News* 17 November 1887.
14. *West Australian* 25 November 1887; *Daily News* 25 November 1887.
15. *Daily News* 1 December 1887.
16. *West Australian* 23 December 1887.
17. Ibid.
18. H. G. Cowin, *The Williams* (Perth: Sands & McDougall 1971), p. 116.
19. *Inquirer* 5 June 1889.
20. Ibid 14 June 1889.

Chapter fourteen

1890-1900

During the 1880s payable gold was at last discovered in Western Australia. The first major finds were in the Kimberley district, then in 1887, while Joe and Wroth were squabbling in Perth, the magic metal was found some 320 kilometres to the eastward in the High-clere Hills by prospectors Anstey, Payne and Greaves. The hills had been distantly sighted and named by Surveyor-General John Septimus Roe in 1836 but had retained their secret for more than half a century. If only Roe had visited the area and discovered its potential. The colony's early struggle for survival would have been so eased that transportation of convicts may never have been considered. The name Moondyne Joe might never have been included in our folklore.

The first discoveries of payable gold led to other finds in the area, including Golden Valley and Southern Cross. Gold was struck at the latter place on 14 January 1888 by Tom Riseley and Mick Toomey who named their find after the constellation that led them to it.[1] After further finds in the general area during the next eight months, the Yilgarn Goldfield was proclaimed on 1 October 1888.[2] 'Yilgarn' was an Aboriginal word for the white quartz with which the area abounded. Within twelve months Southern Cross was established as the centre of the Yilgarn Goldfield and the town's progress was meteoric. Rough bush humpies and tents sprang up overnight and a continual stream of hopeful goldseekers, amongst whom were Louisa and Joseph Johns, followed Hunt's wells and waterholes east of York.

Exactly when Joe decided to head for the diggings is uncertain, though he was in Southern Cross as early as 1891. At over sixty years of age he was apparently undaunted by the arduous nature of the journey. The trip must have brought back many memories. One of the watering places along the hot and dusty trail was Boodalin Soak, where Bugg, James and himself had been captured by Constable Hayden some twenty-four years previously. If Joe was dreaming of finding the fortune in gold promised in O'Reilly's novel, perhaps he should have paused longer at Boodalin Soak. In 1910 the area was noticed to be likely looking gold-bearing country by Alfred Weston who with his brother did some prospecting there.

21 Southern Cross in the 1890s

Their discoveries created a small rush, and by 1915 Westonia was a busy place.[3] But like all the others in those early days, Joe pushed on to Southern Cross, unaware of the fortune beneath his feet.

Upon their arrival at the boom town Louisa and Joe settled down to life in a tent. Jobs for a man with Joe's experience would not have been hard to find, though where he worked and what he did is unknown. Certainly it was not long before he was again involved in a petty controversy.

In September 1891 a man named James Curry reported that a camp oven had been stolen from him.[4] Suspicion fell on Joe and a warrant to search his tent was obtained. The search was carried out by Constable McCarthy, a camp oven was duly found, and on the 24th Joe attended the police court charged with being in unlawful possession of the article. The court was presided over by Michael Finnerty, the gold warden and resident magistrate, who promptly dismissed the case. Apparently there was no basis to Curry's claims and later records show that he was a troublesome character. Under the rough justice dispensed in the makeshift courthouse Curry was once prohibited from having grog for twelve months as the result of a drinking offence. There can be little doubt that such a sentence was considered far more severe than fines or imprisonment. In the shimmering goldfields heat, grog was a comfort and drowner of sorrows for many disillusioned fossickers, therefore to be unable to buy a drink in any of the towns booming hotels was hard punishment indeed.

Louisa and Joe must have witnessed many exciting events during the early years of Southern Cross. On 20 November 1891 David Lindsay and the officers of the Elder Exploring Expedition entered the town and were excitedly welcomed.[5] They had left Adelaide seven months previously and crossed the formidable Great Victoria Desert. Lindsay was astounded to come across the bustling town of Southern Cross since it appeared on none of his maps and he and his men had expected many more miles of wilderness before they reached the fringes of civilization. The party were feted and shown over the mines, and three days later brought their whole camel train through the town. Everybody turned out to cheer them on their way and champagne and speeches flowed in the dining-room of the hotel.

In February 1892 the telegraph line reached Southern Cross but no telegraph office had yet been erected. Undaunted, Mr Harvey, the telegraphist, sat in the street under an umbrella taking and sending messages.[6] In March the first Yilgarn Road Board members were elected, and such was the phenomenal growth of the place, that Southern Cross was declared a municipality some six months later. On September 17 that year the following telegram was dictated by the Southern Cross police for transmission to the Commissioner:

> Arthur Baley arrived here this morning with six hundred ounces gold which he and Ford found one hundred and twenty miles Eastward. Baley says he got one hundred and thirty ounces one Evening — nocked it out of Large Bowlers with Tomahawke — is sure getting two or three thousand ounces in same place — came in in two days — good track — water scarce on the field — four men on the field when he left.[7]

Bayley and Ford had made their stupendous discovery at a place called Coolgardie, a name soon known throughout the world. Within days Southern Cross was all but deserted as a cavalcade of hopeful goldseekers headed for the new field. Excitement over the rich new find prevailed throughout the colony, and it was reported that everyone in Perth and Fremantle seemed to be 'either carrying tents, picks, shovels, and dishes, or otherwise preparing for the road.'[8] Whether Joe tried his luck along with the rest is unknown. Perhaps the exhilaration of just being present during those stirring times was enough.

Life on the goldfields in those days was especially hard for women: the heat, flies, dust and primitive conditions must have taken their toll on Louisa. In April 1893 Joe stood sadly, bushman's hat in hand, at the side of his wife's grave. She had stuck by his side faithfully for fourteen long years, sharing the rough pioneering life her husband chose to follow. She had died suddenly of apoplexy in her fortieth year and her passing must have been a shock to Joe.[9]

Less than a week later Joe was in trouble again.[10] He was brought before Resident Magistrate Finnerty, this time accused of illegally detaining certain property valued at £48 and belonging to Arthur Granville Adams. Again Finnerty dismissed the case against Joe and he went free. Further records of his experiences at Southern Cross have not been found, hence it is presumed that he left the area soon afterwards—a sad and lonely man.

Joe took up residence at Kelmscott again. The long years of hardship and dodging now began to have a marked effect on his mind and his actions grew increasingly erratic. Accused of being unlawfully in possession of a plough, he worked up a real hate against those who had given evidence against him: Higgins, Denning and Taylor.[11] During July 1896 the police were concerned over the production of counterfeit coins in the Kelmscott area, and Joe sent word to them that he had information to give. When Constable Warnecke met Joe, he learned that five 1-shilling pieces, two half-crowns and a broken mould were hidden near Higgin's hut.

'How do you know they're there?', asked the constable.

'Because I put them there', said Joe, producing a shilling mould from his pocket. 'This', he continued, holding up the mould, 'I am going to put in Denning's chaffcutter.'

The poor old fellow's mind was obviously wandering to make such a statement, and Warnecke, quickly snatching the mould from his hand, asked whether Joe expected him to arrest two innocent men.

'You wouldn't arrest me', said Joe.

'Wouldn't I?' asked Warnecke.

Joe stepped back, drew a knife from his pocket and said: 'Before I'll do a lagging for that I'll cut my throat.' He then demanded the mould back but Warnecke turned on his heel and left, remarking that Joe could please himself about cutting his throat.

Warnecke returned the next morning accompanied by Corporal Duncan and Joe was taken into custody. He was charged with being in unlawful possession of a shilling mould and appeared in the Perth Police Court two days later when he was remanded for eight days. The press garbled his name into 'James Moonden',[12] but the police were well aware of his true identity and his past record. All requests for bail were firmly refused.

When the case was prosecuted by Subinspector Lemon on August 13, Joe's counsel, Mr W. Smith, put forward the defence that the wording of the Coinage Act referred only to England and Wales. He argued that the act did not apply locally and therefore his client could not be prosecuted under it. Nonplussed, the police magistrate, Mr J. Cowan, ordered a further remand and again refused bail.[13]

The case was resumed on August 21 when Cowan gave it as his opinion that the Coinage Act did apply in Australia. The crown solicitor, he added, was also of that opinion. Smith, now assisted by a solicitor named Brown, argued in vain. Their objection was noted but the case proceeded with little or no further action from the defence. When the mould was produced in court to be identified by Constable Warnecke, Brown was moved to remark: 'Bah! That's a mould for making buttons for the Salvation Army.' There were no further comments until after the prosecution witnesses had been heard. Then Smith addressed the Bench. He described Constable Warnecke's uncorroborated evidence as a 'cock-and-bull-story'. Cowan retorted that he thought it sufficient for a jury to convict on, whereupon Smith reserved his defence and sat down. The police magistrate ruled that Joe be committed for trial at the next quarterly criminal sessions of the Supreme Court and the old man was returned to the lockup.[14]

When the next criminal sittings of the Supreme Court opened on October 7, Joe's name was not included in the list of cases to be heard.[15] The exact details are uncertain but it appears that he had been released and was never brought to trial. The reason for this seems to be that Smith's argument on August 13 was valid. In fact Queen Victoria had rectified the loophole on August 1. Her amendment to the Coinage Act extended it to apply to the Colonies of New South Wales, South Australia, Tasmania, New Zealand, Victoria, Queensland and Western Australia, but the amendment did not become effective until proclaimed by the governor of each possession. In Western Australia the proclamation was not published until November 1896.[16] Since this was some months too late to apply to Joe, the crown solicitor no longer had a case to put forward. The charges were dropped and Joe went free once more.

The movements of the aging bushranger over the next few years are obscure. He rated a mention in Kimberly's *History of Western Australia*, published in 1897, but the reference was hardly complimentary. Kimberly wrote: 'Many remarkable stories are told of the exploits of another ex-prisoner, "Moondyne Joe". A book has been written with him as a noble hero, and romance and myth encompass him about. But Moondyne was not so great as some of his contemporaries and he obtained credit for exploits which he did not deserve.

He was a successful prison-breaker, but not such an ingenious one as others. In brief he was an overrated celebrity.' How Joe would have fumed if he had read the historian's past-tense comments on his career.

On 26 January 1900 Joe was found wandering aimlessly around South Perth by Constable Mason who considered him to be of unsound mind.[17] The pathetic old man, alone and unwanted, was charged at the Perth Court of Petty Sessions on the following day and Justices Haynes and Russell ordered him to the Mount Eliza Invalid Depot for medical treatment. These buildings, tucked between Mounts Bay Road and the foot of Mount Eliza on the Perth side of the brewery, had originally been constructed as a convict depot. It will be recalled that Joe had been discharged to that depot in 1864 and it is likely that he had spent some time there as a convict on other occasions. Now, as a confused old man, it is possible that he never realized that the buildings no longer served their original purpose. All the old stubbornness and outrage at what he considered injustice seems to have returned.

After only eleven days at the depot he absconded. Recaptured by Constable Hickey and returned before the Court of Petty Sessions, he was ordered to return to the depot for further treatment. This time he stayed twelve days. He was caught once more, taken before the Court of Petty Sessions once more and once more ordered back to the depot. Another twelve days and again he got out. By this time both the police and the court were heartily sick and tired of his seemingly senseless behaviour. On 6 March 1900 he was sentenced to one month in Fremantle Prison without hard labour. For Joe, now aged about seventy-two, this was the beginning of the end.

That same day he was taken down to Fremantle, where once more he saw the inside of those hated walls.[18] His already frail condition deteriorated rapidly. He spent a day in the prison hospital on March 8,[19] and then on the 13th he was again put into the hospital. He stayed there for the remainder of his sentence. On the 19th Dr James Hope put the patient under treatment for mental disorder, which was continued up until his release. The treatment, whatever it was, does not seem to have been particularly successful because on April 6 when Joe was released, the doctor recommended that the police be advised of the state of the old-fellow's mind.

22 The Fremantle Lunatic Asylum, where Joe died on 13 August 1900.
Now the Fremantle Museum and Arts Centre

Joe did not improve. He ended his days in the Fremantle Lunatic
Asylum (now the Fremantle Museum and Arts Centre) on 13 August
1900.[20] Dr Hope gave the cause of death as senile dementia. On
August 16 Joe was buried in a pauper's grave in the Fremantle
Cemetery.[21] Arthur E. Davies undertook the arrangements and men
named Jarvis and McDonough witnessed the burial. Nobody seems
to have been present who knew Joe and the service was conducted
by Mr Saunders, a Church of England minister. Joe had made his
last escape, but his story does not end with his death. His name was
legend, and in some ways his death was only the beginning.

REFERENCES

1. P. T. McMahon, *They Wished Upon a Star* (Perth: Service Printing
    Co. 1972).
2. Malcolm A. C. Fraser, *Western Australian Year Book 1902-04,* p. 833.
3. *West Australian* 12 April 1947.
4. Police Records, WAA Acc. No. 415: Southern Cross Occurrence Book.

5. David Lindsay, *Journal of the Elder Exploring Expedition 1891* (Adelaide: Government Printer 1893).
6. *Southern Cross Herald* 3 August 1894.
7. Police Records, WAA Acc. No. 415: Southern Cross Occ. Book.
8. *West Australian* 21 September 1892.
9. Death Certificate 442/1893, Registrar General's Office.
10. Police Records, WAA Acc. No. 415: Southern Cross Occ. Book.
11. *Western Mail* 28 August 1896.
12. *Daily News* 28 July 1896.
13. Ibid 13 August 1896.
14. Ibid 21 August 1896.
15. Ibid 6 October 1896.
16. *Government Gazette* 13 November 1896.
17. Mary Tamblyn, Research in 1968, WAA 2086A.
18. Convict Records, WAA Acc. No. 1156 R&D13B.
19. Ibid M25B.
20. Death Certificate 983/1900, Registrar General's Office.
21. Mary Tamblyn, Research in 1968, WAA 2086A.

Chapter fifteen

Ever since Joe's bushranging days the name Moondyne, mentioned wherever men gathered and yarned, would bring forth a host of stories. The stories rarely lost in the telling and most were embellished and refined each time they were retold. Great care has been taken in the preceeding chapters to exclude any information that was not supported by contemporary sources or actual eye-witness accounts. Unfortunately this method leaves gaps in Joe's life but, strangely, the many uncorroborated tales of his exploits do little to fill such gaps. In spite of this there are several popular legends that are worthy of discussion. (Naturally, all the yarns cannot be included in this work, if only for the simple reason that many of them remain unknown to the author.)

From conversations during the compiling of material for this book it became apparent that a great many people were under the impression that Joe was either Aboriginal or at least part-Aboriginal. This myth is shown to be false in the main text, and although Joe's exact birthplace is still a matter of conjecture, the fact that Johns is a common Welsh surname coupled with his arrest in Wales, gives rise to the assumption that Joe was Welsh. Some Welshmen have a dark swarthy complexion, therefore it has been suggested that such a complexion could have begun the tale that Joe was of Aboriginal descent. This argument falls apart when it is recalled that official descriptions state that his complexion was 'sallow'.[1] The real origin of the myth probably lies in the name by which he was (and still is) best known, that is 'Moondyne Joe'. Another factor may have been his uncanny ability to outwit the best native trackers in the colony. Whatever the case, there is no doubt that Joe was European and it is a fair assumption to say that he was Welsh. The latter will not be positively proved without an expensive and time-consuming search of records in Great Britain.

Deprived of the story that Joe was Aboriginal, many people will say that he lived with the Aborigines. There is not a scrap of contemporary evidence to support this and it could be fobbed off as a direct result of O'Reilly's fantasy. Or does the story really apply to Frank Hall whose short but spectacular bushranging career had the whole colony talking? Hall is known to have had the complete confidence of the south-west tribes and lived with them frequently.[2] He was recognized as being as good, if not better, in the bush than Joe. But between 1855 and 1861 nothing is known of Joe's way of life, except that in the latter year he was living in a hut at Moondyne Spring and trapping horses at little-known springs and soaks along the Avon valley. He was recognized as 'a thorough bushman' even then, although how and where he learnt his bushmanship is a matter for speculation. It is entirely possible that his knowledge came from the Aborigines, but unfortunately there seems to be no way of proving the case one way or the other.

Much has been written of Joe since his death and some writers have given the impression that he was Western Australia's 'only' bushranger.[3] The exploits of a good many of Western Australia's bushrangers were deliberately included in the main text of this book to show the absurdity of such a notion. It would be more correct to say that Joe was Western Australia's best-known bushranger.

Another idea put forward is that Joe was not a 'real' bushranger.[4] Presumably this means that Western Australia had no 'real' bush-rangers, such a heritage belonging exclusively to the eastern states.

This is ridiculous. By what yardstick do we measure a 'real' bush-ranger? Must they have killed a certain number of people, stolen a certain amount of gold bullion, held up a certain number of mail coaches, or do they only become 'real' when a television play is based on their lives? The word bushranging sprang from the habits of escapees during Australia's convict days: they 'ranged the bush'. Modern dictionaries give the meaning of bushranger as a lawless person, often an escaped criminal, who takes to the bush and lives by robbery. Nothing could describe Joe and his contemporaries in Western Australia more exactly.

Many of the myths about Joe concern escapes. According to one story Joe possessed a pony which he fed well on oats.[5] When an unbranded brumby ate the oats, Joe shot it. In those days wild horses were frequently shot as nuisances but a special licence was required, a licence that Joe did not possess. He is said to have been arrested at Newcastle on a charge of unlawfully killing a horse and thrown into the lockup at Toodyay. Considering the charge to be unjust, Joe escaped, taking with him the warder's pistol, a serious offence. Not one word of this incident appears in the detailed Police and Convict Depot Occurrence Books of the area, and the story appears to be nothing more than a completely garbled version of his 1861 escape.

A popular misconception concerning that 1861 escape is that Joe took off on Resident Magistrate Durlacher's horse. This appears to have originated from Durlacher's letter to the colonial secretary (see Chapter Three), but if that letter is read carefully, it is clear that Durlacher does not lay claim to the animal. He writes: 'a horse and my saddle and bridle'. In fact, because of a shortage of police horses Durlacher had loaned his mount to Constable Keane's native assistant and these two are known to have been away searching Joe's huts at Moondyne at the time of the escape. This explains how the resident magistrate's brand new saddle and bridle came to be hang-ing in the police stable, surely an unusual circumstance. Before departing for Moondyne hills Keane's native assistant would have placed his own saddle and bridle on Durlacher's horse and carefully hung Durlacher's gleaming equipment from the wall. No doubt Joe was suitably impressed by the quality of equipment available on the night of his escape. From the abundant police reports on the subject it is obvious that the horse stolen that night was the one Joe had previously been accused of stealing. This was invariably referred to as 'the property of some person or persons unknown', and was definitely not Durlacher's.

Another erroneous idea is that Joe made that escape from the present old Gaol Museum at Toodyay, but that building, originally called the 'Newcastle Lockup', was not completed until 1864. In fact Joe's 1861 escape was an important factor that led to the construction of this substantial stone building. It is sometimes called 'the gaol they built for Joe', although there is no record that he was ever held in its cells. Despite this a booklet available at the Old Gaol Museum states that he used a table fork to scratch away mortar from between the stones in a cell there. After removing the stones he is supposed to have crawled out and hidden in the resident magistrate's hay loft while the police scoured the town and surrounding country for him. This tale is not supported by contemporary records.

Perhaps the best known escape myth concerns the Old Mahogany Inn on the Great Eastern Highway. There are several versions of this tale and one has it that the inn was Joe's 'hideout'.[6] When the police found out and came to arrest him, Joe squeezed through the attic window, slid down the roof onto a policeman's horse and galloped away. It is extremely doubtful that any publican would have risked his licence and livelihood to hide a bushranger, and the complete and detailed police records of the period show that suspicion never once fell on the owners of the inn at Mahogany Creek. No police officer ever had his horse stolen from there, but still the tale persists. One writer has even embellished the tale by stating that Joe was visiting a maid at the inn when the police arrived and prompted his spectacular getaway.[7] This version appears to have been taken straight from the tales about highwayman Dick Turpin.

The story of Joe's escape from the inn was first published in the *Western Australian Historical Society Journal* of 1929. The tale was included in an article by Mrs T. Pelloe on the history of the York road. Over sixty years after the alleged event Mrs Pelloe interviewed several old teamsters who told her that Joe was recognized when drinking at Horton's Inn at 'The Lakes'. The landlord drugged his ale and sent for the police. When the latter arrived, Joe recovered quickly and fought hard for his liberty. It took five men to hold and handcuff him. For some reason the police stopped at Mahogany Creek on their way back to Guildford, and there Joe slipped his handcuffs, took his own horse from among the police mounts and galloped away to the Avon valley and his beloved Moondyne hills. This is a lucid and logical story. Apart from the drugged ale (the grog of those days hardly required the assistance of drugs) the story seemed quite believable but research proved conclusively that Joe took part in no such escapade.

Why then would the teamsters relate such a story? The answer appears to be that they confused and combined the details of James Lilly's capture at Horton's Inn (see Chapter Two) and the escape of John Thomas from the inn at Mahogany Creek (see Chapter Four) and applied the resulting tale to Joe. This is a very typical example of the distortion that can occur in stories told and retold over a long period, and is one of the main reasons why not even the most plausible of such stories have been included in the main text of this book.

Other escape stories exist, notably about Joe's alleged escapes from the old gaols at Perth and York. Neither of these tales are based on fact and both are completely unsupported by historical research. The latter is of extremely recent origin and stems from a 're-enactment' staged at the 1975 York Fair. It is ironic that the York Society, a body dedicated to the preservation of history, should have been responsible for such a distortion. Thousands of visitors to York saw Joe, his 'girlfriend' (?) and gang fight a running gun battle with the police across York's rooftops. A letter from the author, protesting about the historical inaccuracy and sensationalism of the 're-enactment' appeared in the *West Australian* on 11 October 1975. The York Society defended itself by citing the use of 'poetic license' and stating that many legends were included in the book *Moondyne* by John Boyle O'Reilly 'who escaped from Fremantle after serving time with Moondyne'. Leaving aside the fact that O'Reilly mentioned nothing concerning an escape from the York gaol, it is a common belief that the Irishman got his information from the horse's mouth. Since Joe had made his escape through the wall of Fremantle Prison before O'Reilly arrived in the Colony and was not recaptured until after O'Reilly had gone into hiding, this is hardly likely. The author was present at the opening of the 1975 York Fair and, in all fairness to the York Society, was pleased to hear it explained to the audience that the re-enactment was not based on fact. On the other hand, one wonders what made the most impression on the youngsters who were present, the opening speech or the stunt men with blazing guns leaping from rooftop to rooftop.

One yarn that was popular for many years concerned Joe's most spectacular escape from Fremantle Prison in March 1867. It was said that Joe crossed the new bridge over the Swan River at Fremantle on the night before it was to be officially opened by Governor Hampton. Apart from the fact that Joe's escape was made in broad daylight, there appears to be no evidence that Governor Hampton ever attended an official opening ceremony. As early as December 1864, when only the first six piles had been driven, the *Inquirer* had made public the governor's ambition to drive over the bridge 'four-in-hand' before he left the colony.[8] He realized his ambition on 14 November 1866 and the bridge was thrown open for general traffic one week later.[9] On the night after this a small unofficial ceremony took place but the governor was not present. In January 1867 the Fremantle Town Trust composed a memorial to the governor which was signed by many of the town's inhabitants. The missive thanked Governor Hampton for allowing the use of the bridge before its final completion and prayed that His Excellency would appoint a day for an opening ceremony.[10] His Excellency's willingness was made public soon afterwards,[11] but he and Mrs Hampton left for an extended holiday on Rottnest Island almost immediately,[12] and after their return the matter appears to have been forgotten.

One explanation for this myth has been put forward by Alexandra Hasluck in her book *Unwilling Emigrants*. Lady Hasluck suggests that Joe could have forestalled the governor in crossing the almost completed bridge when he was returned to gaol in October 1866. That trip was made with all possible speed. Joe, Bugg and James were bundled into a cart at York at 9.00 am on October 8.[13] They reached Guildford at 11.30 pm that night and were at Fremantle three and a half hours later.[14] Lady Hasluck's theory is that they went via Perth, and instead of using the ferry at Fremantle, crossed the bridge, when Joe may have quipped to his escort that he had beaten the governor. As the ferry would hardly have been available at 3 o'clock in the morning, this explanation must remain a possibility, but is it logical to assume that the police took that route? Substantial bridges spanned both the Helena and Canning Rivers and they could have travelled between Guildford and Fremantle without crossing the Swan. Unfortunately it seems as if this question, like so many others applying to Joe's life, may never be answered satisfactorily.

A great deal of mystery also surrounds Joe's hideouts. Since he was almost continually on the move in the bush, the idea of one permanent hideout must be abandoned. It can be safely assumed that he camped near almost every spring on the tributaries of the Avon River between Toodyay and the coastal plain. A pamphlet on the Young Australia League resort Araluen states that Joe resided at a spot called 'Moondyne Hollow' during his two years' period of freedom from 1867 to 1869. The hollow in question is not far east of Kelmscott, where Joe had friends, and it is quite possible that he sometimes camped there. The suggestion that he lived there for the whole two years' period is proven wrong by the reports mentioned in Chapters Nine, Ten and Eleven.

Other stories imply that the Old Mahogany Inn at Mahogany Creek and the Rose and Crown Hotel at Guildford were used as hideouts by Joe.[15] As before stated, it is hard to imagine any publican risking his licence to harbour a fugitive from the law. The Old Mahogany Inn was visited regularly by police on escort duty and the Rose and Crown is only a stone's throw from the old Guildford police station. Both places appear highly unlikely as hideouts although it is possible that Joe frequented these inns in later life as a paying customer. He is reputed to have worked as a yardman for a time at the Old Mahogany Inn but the story is unsubstantiated by contemporary evidence.

A link with Joe seems to assure publicity for any hotel in the hills. Some brand new 'legends' were included in an article on the Parkerville Tavern published in November 1976.[16] It was implied that the old hotel had been one of Joe's haunts, that he used the cellar as a hideout and that he could have buried some of his 'loot' there. Since Parkerville's first hotel was not licensed until March 1902 such tales are obviously absurd.

Almost any cave in the Darling Range will be promoted as 'Moondyne Joe's hideout', and it is fortunate that caves are rare in granite country. Mostly such caves, if they can be called that, consist of one boulder resting on others. They rarely make particularly good shelters and it is doubtful that Joe used a cave regularly as a hideout even though such stories are legion. Moondyne Cave near Augusta is often said to be a hideout of Joe's, but as he was never on the run from the police when residing at Karridale, his need for a hideout in that quarter would hardly be pressing.

It has sometimes been suggested that an old mask of oriental design displayed in the Historical Society's museum at Nedlands was worn by Joe. Research has indicated that Joe never wore a mask during his bushranging days. On 13 June 1977 the Council of the Royal Western Australian Historical Society carried a motion stating 'that, as the iron mask at Stirling House was not owned or used by Moondyne Joe, no member of the Historical Society is permitted to so describe it or to display it or to use photographs or drawings of it'. This sensible act should prevent any further misrepresentation of that particular item.

Another myth concerns Joe's attitude towards guns. Several writers have stated that he never had a gun, never stole one, in fact never even knew how to use one.[17] Why then did he say so many times that he would be all right in the bush with a gun and a 'roo dog? Who shot the stolen horse in 1861? Was Mrs Martin mistaken when under oath in 1865 she recalled loaning Joe a gun? Was Thomas Reynolds lying when he told Hayden that the taller of the two men who held him up had the gun? (The men were Joe, 1.80 metre [5 feet 10¾ inches], and David Evans, 1.62 metre [5 feet, 3¾ inches].) After stealing two guns from Everett's store in 1866, why did Joe, Bugg and James steal a third gun from Roser's? (See Chapter Eight and Appendix C.) Although upset by his poor aim on one occasion, Frances Brockman clearly indicates that it was Joe who killed beef at Wallcliffe while he lived there. From this it can be assumed that his aim was not habitually bad. There can be no doubt that Joe both stole and used guns during his bushranging career, but they were invariably used for survival rather than war-fare with the police. It is possible that he never actually owned a gun, although even that is doubtful. A gun would have been a particularly useful item during his horse-trapping days.

One of the most persistent myths has Joe in a drunken stupor when captured at Ferguson's cellars. This was refuted by Ferguson himself in 1928,[18] and by Canon Burton in 1943,[19] but still the tale is told. There is every chance that Joe was far from teetotal, nevertheless the fact remains that Ferguson and party discovered him in the cellar before he was able to sample the contents.

A legend of some interest concerns Joe's activities at Karridale. He is reputed to have discovered a strange jinker on M. C. Davies's timber leases. Valuable trees had been stolen from the area before but Joe ended the thefts by sawing through the spokes of the huge wheels on the thief's jinker. There are several slightly different versions of this tale, but it may well be based on fact. Unfortunately the details are vague and the non-existance of a contemporary report renders it difficult to comment on the authenticity of the story. Similar difficulties exist in evaluating many of the stories concerning Joe's later life.

The death of Western Australia's best known bushranger passed unnoticed at the time but the event has not escaped latter-day confusion. In 1929, he was said to have passed away a few years previously at the Old Men's Depot in Claremont.[20] This was repeated by many of the historians who later wrote about Joe's escapades. The date gradually became more specific, changing from a vague '1920s' to a positive '1920'. The record was set straight by Mary Tamblyn's research in 1968, the results of which were published in the *Australian Dictionary of Biography*. Strangely the facts are still ignored by some writers who state that Joe died at the Sunset Old Men's Home in Dalkeith. Like most persistent myths, the tale may be based partly on fact. Early in 1976 the late Superintendent Charles Pollard recalled an incident that took place early in his police career. The Cottesloe police were requested to remove an old derelict from a humpie near the beach and place him in an institution. The old fellow's mind was wandering and he told the police that he was Moondyne Joe. Of course his story was not true, but if such a fellow made a death-bed claim to be Moondyne Joe in a nursing home at Claremont or Dalkeith in the 1920s, the reason for the confusion amongst historians would become plain. In any case the date of Joe's death has now been established beyond doubt as 13 August 1900.

One thing is certain. Joe will never be forgotten. The old stories will continue to be told. Speculation about the unknown periods of his life will cause new stories to spring up and these will grow and change with the passing years. That is always the way when a man becomes a legend. Joe's way of life and determination to be free have a romantic appeal that cannot be ignored, and as 'Moondyne Joe' he will forever retain his place in the heritage of the State of Western Australia.

REFERENCES

1. Convict Records, WAA Acc. No. 1156 R4.
2. Exploration Diaries, vol. 5, pp. 204-330.
3. Canon A. Burton, *The Story of the Swan District* (Perth: John Muhling 1938), p. 55; *West Australian* 13 August, 10 October 1975.
4. Athole Stewart, 'Western Sussex', *Early Days,* vol. 10, December 1948, p. 32.
5. Rica Erickson, *Old Toodyay and Newcastle,* p. 201.
6. *The Darling* (Holiday Special) December 1975.
7. *West Australian* 13 August 1975.
8. *Inquirer* 25 January 1865.
9. John K. Ewers, *The Western Gateway,* 2nd rev. edn (Nedlands: University of Western Australia Press 1971), p. 54.
10. Governor's Correspondence, 9 January 1867, WAA Acc. No. 136.
11. *Perth Gazette* 18 January 1867.
12. *Fremantle Herald* 2 February, 9 March 1867.
13. Police Records, WAA Acc. No. 371 5.
14. *Perth Gazette* 12 October 1866.
15. *The Darling* (Holiday Special) December 1975; *West Australian* 4 October 1975.
16. *West Australian* 4 November 1976 (East Suburban Section), p. 14.
17. *South Western News* 8 April 1932; Alexandra Hasluck, *Unwilling Emigrants* (Melbourne: Oxford University Press 1959), p. 66.
18. *Sunday Times* 25 May 1928.
19. Burton, *The Story of the Swan District.*
20. W. C. Thomas, 'Outlines of the Timber Industry', *Early Days,* vol. 1, part 5, p. 34.

Appendixes

APPENDIX A

List of articles stolen from the premises of James Everett. (WAA Acc. No. 129 9/778)

One gold watch guard marked 100
Two double-barrelled guns
3 lbs of gum
Twenty boxes of gun caps
25 lbs of gun shot
Five or six white shirts
Three or four striped shirts
Three of four black silk kerchiefs
Eight pairs of moleskin trousers
Thirty-six ladies fancy kerchiefs
Four men's fancy neck kerchiefs
Four pairs of patent leather garters
One pair of light elastic-sided boots
One pair of light lace-up boots
One pair of light lace-up nailed boots
Some blue serge material
Some moleskin material
$1\frac{1}{4}$ lbs of black thread and silk twist
One cloth overcoat
One dark-green striped overcoat

One dark tweed overcoat with a velvet collar
One black cloth coat
Two pairs of black cloth trousers
One pair of striped tweed trousers
One black cloth waistcoat
Two buff waistcoats
One light tweed cap
Forty boxes of matches
Four new butchers knives
Some candles
One large pair of scissors
One dark-green pocket book with an elastic fastener
Six or seven W.A. bank notes
One sovereign
16 lbs of tobacco
One pair of large blankets
Five tins of preserved salmon
Sundry other provisions
Half a bottle of strychnine

APPENDIX B

List of articles recovered from the bush by James Everett. (WAA Acc. No. 422 Vol. 2)

Two new tweed coats
One pair of black cloth trousers
Six patent leather belts
Two pieces of moleskin
One hide of calfskin and several pieces
20 lbs of bacon

APPENDIX C

List of articles found on the absconders by Sergeant Kelly. (WAA Acc. No. 129 9/912)

7 lbs of powder
Three pairs of leggings
One pocket-book
Three pairs of boots
One black silk handkerchief
Two white shirts
One white guernsey
Three cotton shirts
One pair of drawers
One buff-corded vest
Three leather water bottles
One patent leather belt
Three pairs of trousers (moleskin)
Three blue serge smocks
One pack of cards
Three small lots of tea
Twelve boxes of gun caps
Three lots of gun shot
A large quantity of black and white thread
Three large iron spoons
Twenty-two sticks of tobacco
One shot belt
Three carpenter's pencils
Eleven boxes of matches
Three knots of whipcord
Three looking glasses
One silk pocket handkerchief
Two nutmegs
One box of writing pens
One razor
One tweed cap
Three coats
Two double-barrelled guns
One gold watch guard
One compass
Seven fancy neckties
Four wires of writing paper

All the above identified and claimed by James Everett.

One double-barrelled gun
One pair of boots
One dog

All the above identified and claimed by William Roser.

One revolver
One pistol flask

The above belonging to William Dodd.

Bibliography

Manuscript records and documents

At the Western Australian State Archives (WAA), Battye Library, Perth

Convict Records, WAA Acc. No. 1156: items C32, C48, C49, C50, C52, M25B, OCC2, R1B, R4, R7, R13, R20, R21B, R26, R&D4, R&D5, R&D13B, SO12, V14, V23A; Acc. No. 128: *Racehorse* muster list.
Correspondence from the Resident Magistrate at Newcastle to the Colonial Secretary, WAA CSO487, CSO583.
Death Certificates, numbers 442/1893 and 983/1900 filed in the Registrar-General's Office, Perth.
Exploration Diaries, vols 5 and 6, WAA.
Governor's Correspondence, WAA Acc. No. 136.
Original Plans Swan 131 and Resumptions 347. Lands Department Plan Room, Perth.
Police Records, WAA Acc. No. 129: Report dated 8 Nov. 1860 and items 2/236, 2/655, 2/745, 3/812, 3/891, 5/901, 5/966, 6/58, 8/426, 8/450, 8/464, 8/499, 8/536, 9/615, 9/649, 9/668, 9/719, 9/744, 9/750, 9/778, 9/802, 9/912, 10/463, 11/732, 12/922, 12/958; Acc. No. 371: items 4 and 5; Acc. No. 415: Southern Cross Occurrence Book; Acc. No. 422: vols 1 and 2.

Published sources

Battye, J. S. *Western Australia: A History from its Discovery to the Inauguration of the Commonwealth.* London: Oxford University Press 1924

Burton, Canon [A]. *The Story of the Swan District.* Perth: John Muhling 1938.

Cowin, H. G. *The Williams.* Perth: Sands & McDougall Pty Ltd 1971.

Erickson, Rica. *Old Toodyay and Newcastle.* Perth: Toodyay Shire Council 1974.

Ewers, John K. *The Western Gateway.* 2nd rev. edn. Nedlands: University of Western Australia Press 1971.

Fraser, Malcolm A. C. *Western Australian Year Book 1902-04.* 13th edn. Perth: Government Printer 1906.

Hasluck, Alexandra. *Unwilling Emigrants.* Melbourne: Oxford University Press 1959.

Lindsay, David. *Journal of the Elder Exploring Expedition 1891.* Adelaide: Government Printer 1893.

Martin, James and Panter, Frederick Kennedy. *Journals and Reports of Two Voyages to the Glenelg River and the North-West Coast of Australia 1863-4.* Perth: A. Shenton 1864.

McMahon, P. T. *They Wished Upon a Star.* Perth: Service Printing Co. Pty Ltd 1972.

Millett, (Mrs) Edward. *An Australian Parsonage.* London: E. Stanford 1872.

Mitchell, Samuel. *Looking Backward, Reminiscences of 42 Years.* Geraldton Newspapers Ltd Print 1970.

O'Reilly, John Boyle. *Moondyne.* New York: P. J. Kennedy 1879.

Panter, Frederick Kennedy. (See Martin, James.)

Pike, Douglas. *Australian Dictionary of Biography.* Vol. 5. Carlton: Melbourne University Press 1974.

Reilly, J. T. *Reminiscences of Fifty Years Residence in Western Australia.* Perth: Sands & McDougall 1901.

Roche, James Jeffrey. *Life, Poems and Speeches of John Boyle O'Reilly.* New York: Cassel Publishing Co. 1891.

Stewart, Athole. 'Western Sussex', *Early Days, Journal and Proceedings of the Western Australian Historical Society*, vol. 10, December 1948, Perth, Western Australian Historical Society.

Thomas, W. C. 'Outlines of the Timber Industry', *Early Days*, vol. 1, pt 5, 1929.

Treadgold, C. 'Bushrangers in Western Australia', *Early Days*, vol. 2, October 1939.

Watson, John. *Catalpa 1876.* Perth: John Watson 1976.

The Western Australian Almanac and Directory for 1879. Perth: Stirling Bros 1879.

Western Australian Government Gazette, 1849-96.

Newspapers (Western Australia)

Daily News
Fremantle Herald
Herald
Hereford Times (England)
Inquirer
Perth Gazette
South Western News
Southern Cross Herald
Sunday Times
The Darling
West Australian
Western Mail

Unpublished theses and research

Anderson, Peggy. Economic Aspects of Transportation to Western Australia. BA honours thesis, University of Western Australia 1950.

[Brockman, Frances.] Diary of Frances Brockman. WAA 938A, Battye Library, Perth.

[Buckingham, Thomas.] Memoirs of Thomas Buckingham. WAA QB/BUC, Battye Library, Perth.

Carroll, Martin C. Jnr. Behind the Lighthouse. PhD thesis, Dept of English, Iowa State University 1954.

Gertzel, Cherry. The Convict System in Western Australia 1850-1870. BA honours thesis, University of Western Australia 1949.

Jennings, Rodger. The Story of Henry Yelverton of Quindalup. WAA PR767, Battye Library, Perth.

Tamblyn, Mary. Research in 1968. WAA 2086A, Battye Library, Perth.

[Withers, E. H.] Memories of E. H. Withers. WAA HS/574, Battye Library, Perth.

Index

165

Brother John, 100
Brown, John, 94
Brown, Thomas, 78-9
Brown, — , 142
Bruce, Lieutenant-Colonel, 108
Buck, Constable Richard, 42-3, 91
Buckingham, Thomas, 42
Buckskin, Johnny, 69, 71, 93
Bugg, Thomas, 59, 68, 81, 88, 138, 151, 153
Bull Creek, 57, 91
Bullen's Hotel, 131
Bunbury, 9, 35, 43, 104, 116-17, 119, 125
Burns, James, 57
Burnside, Constable Thomas, 20-2, 24-5
Burt, Chief Justice, 24-6
Burton, Canon, 154
Bush Inn, 12, 68, 78-9, 99
Bussell, Alfred, 122-3
Busselton, 31, 35, 104, 116, 121-2, 135
'Butler's Swamp'; *see* Lake Claremont

Camden Harbour, 35
Campbell, Constable, 64, 68, 91, 93
Campbell, Sir Alexander, 13
Canning Bridge, 29, 57-8, 91
Canning River, 13, 15-16, 30-1, 35, 41-2, 44-5, 47-8, 57-8, 91, 93, 103, 131, 152
Capel, 13
Carter, Joseph, 49, 61
Catalpa, 119-20
Cave Hill, 60
Chadwicke, William, 104
Champion, 8
Chauncy Gully, 125
Chepstow, 1
Chidlow, William, 75
'Chidlows Well', 125-6
'Chittering Brook', *see* Brockman River
Christmas, George, 44
Clackline, 65
Claffey, Sergeant, 131-2
Claremont, 154
Clayton, Corporal, 86
Clifton, William John, 86, 116-17

Cockburn Sound, 6, 120, 135
Connor, Detective, 126
Connor, — , 86
Convict Establishment; *see* Fremantle Prison
Cook, Thomas, 19, 23
Cook, — , 44
Cook, — , 95
Coolgardie, 140
Cornish, — , 132
Cottesloe, 154
Cowan, J., 141-2
Cowan, W., 49, 52, 78-9, 83, 118
Cowaramup, 123
Cowle, James, 94
Crampton, — , 95
Crickhowell, 2-3
Cross, William, 2, 4
Cruse's Mill, 67
Curry, James, 139

Dale River, 46
Dale, Sergeant W., 91
Dalkeith, 36, 154
Dandalup, 104
Darling Range, 10, 32, 131-2, 152
Davies, Arthur E., 144
Davies, Maurice C., 123, 154
Davies, Mrs, 130
Deepdale, 65
Denning, — , 141
Dodd, William, 58-61, 69-70, 86
Donnybrook, 116
Doodenanning, 48
Doust, Isaac, 12
Drolf, — , 34
Drummond, — , 64
Duffy, Daniel, 44
Duncan, Corporal, 141
Dunmall, Constable, 45, 58, 91, 93
Durlacher, Alfred, 17, 19-23, 26, 28-9, 59-61, 148
Dyer, Sergeant, 35

Edwards, John, 73
Edwards, Ken, 13

King George Sound, 9
Kingston, Henry, 20-2, 26, 70
Kirk, Constable, 59-61, 65-6, 68-9, 71, 74-5, 77, 101
Knott, — , 70
Kojonup, 34, 43, 105
Koolyanobbing, 47

Lake Claremont, 91, 101
Lake Lefroy, 56
Lake Roe, 76
Lally, Constable Michael, 32, 65-6, 68-9, 71, 77, 79, 107
Landor, — , 24-5
Larwood, Alfred, 75
Lawrence, Subinspector, 131, 133
Leake, G. W., 54, 130
Leander, 8-9
Lee, Constable, 135
Leichardt, Ludwig, 47
Lefroy, Henry Maxwell, 16, 55, 90, 114-15, 118
Lemon, Subinspector, 141
Leschenault Estuary, 31
Lilly, James, 13-16, 31, 150
Lindsay, David, 139
Liverpool, 35
Llanelly, 1-2
Lloyd's Inn; *see* 'Nineteen Mile Inn'
Lockville, 121
Lodge, Inspector, 131
Lossom, Charles, 35

Mahogany Creek, 30, 32, 70, 149-50, 152
'Malgatup', 34
Maloney, Constable, 91
Manaring Lake; *see* 'The Lakes'
Mann, John, 114
Margaret River, 122-3, 135
Martin, H., 65
Martin, Henry, 41-3
Martin, Mrs 42-3, 153
Martin, — , 78
Martinup, 34
Mason, Benjamin, 58, 93
Mason, Constable, 143

Mason, — , 99-100
Mathews, Robert, 74
Mayo, — , 102
McAlinden, Constable, 15
McAtee, Constable, 60-1, 65-9, 71, 73-5, 77-9, 93-4
McCamish, Constable, 91
McCarthy, Constable, 139
McCloud, — , 58
McCormack, Mrs, 42
McDermott, — , 32
McDonald, John. 17
McDonough, — , 144
McGregor, Gavin, 123-5
McKay, Constable, 113
McKeen, — , 33
McKnoe, William, 12, 65
McLarty, — , 129
McMahon, — , 102
McPherson, Duncan, 29
Mead, Henry, 15
Mercer, — , 33
Middleton, — , 30
Millar Bros., 125
Mills, — , 30
Moan, Constable, 60-1
Mokine, 59-60, 65
Monaghan, Constable, 60-4, 79
Monger, Constable, 47
Monger, J. H., 47
Monmouth, 1-2
'Monument Hill', 130
'Moondyne', 12-15, 19, 23, 60-1, 65, 68, 95, 150
Moondyne Brook, 13
Moondyne Cave, 125, 153
'Moondyne Hollow', 152
Moondyne Joe; *see* Johns, Joseph Bolitho
Moondyne Spring, 12-13, 75, 78, 94, 147
Moore, Constable, 94-5
Moore, Peter, 79, 83
Moore, — , 131
Moore River, 107
Morgan, — , 65
Morley, H., 65
Morrill, — , 99-100

172   *Index*